What Readers are Saying...

"As a parent, grandparent, entrepreneur, coach, and consultant, I am inspired by the wisdom of the young people in this book! Whether you are in education, business, or the government sector, you owe it to yourself to discover how *Living The Potential* could be a contribution to you, as well as how you might make a difference in the systems in which you live and work."

Nancy Miriam Hawley, CEO, Enlignment, Inc.
Founder of Systems Perspectives LLC
Co-author of *You and Your Partner, Inc.*
Founder and Co-author of *Our Bodies, Ourselves*

"Renee Beth Poindexter employs facets of her own life story to illustrate humanity's profound need to recognize and nurture the unique gifts and talents that each of us holds—and particularly those of our children and youth. This fascinating book is an eloquent call for the revisioning of our educational system and of the relationship between business and education. *Living The Potential* is a profound and inspiring book! It's also a fascinating read."

David Marshak, Founding President of the
SelfDesign Graduate Institute
Author of *Kids Need the Same Teacher for More than
One Year, Evolutionary Parenting,* and *The Common
Vision: Parenting and Educating for Wholeness*

"*Living The Potential* presents an exciting new vision for education based on the fundamental premise that all students already have the seeds of wisdom within them. This hopeful vision invites all of us to collaborate together to create learning environments that support and sustain students' inner wisdom. We are invited to consider what education would look like if its main focus was unleashing this boundless potential within all students. May this empowering vision based on creativity, collaboration, and cooperation help make a wisdom-based learning the foundation for education throughout the world."

Dr. Dicken Bettinger, EdD
Retired Licensed Clinical Psychologist
Global Seminar Leader in Psychological and Spiritual
Well-being, Author of *Coming Home: Uncovering
the Foundations of Psychological Well-being*

"As a Legacy Mentor for Her Majesty Queen Elizabeth II Diamond Jubilee Queens Young Leaders Program, I see the critical importance of mentoring, teaching, and developing the open thinking of the generations to come, and how vital it will be to those who face real work problems and situations. Renee Beth's approach demands we awaken to the reality that curiosity, creativity, and innovative thinking are our future. Her dedication to advancing education is heartfelt and cutting-edge."

Dr. R.L.R. Bietz, PhD-MBA
Founder of BioRev, LLC, President of Board of
Directors: Univera Serve First
President of Univera, Inc.
Author of *The DNA of Business*

"In *Living The Potential,* Renee Beth Poindexter proves she is a visionary who sees the possibilities of a world yet to be. There lies a pearl of deep and profound wisdom—yet untapped—in the collective soul of our youth; this inherent potential will give birth to a new world beyond our current understanding; and our job is to nurture this potential and bring it forward. Read this book and be teachable—learn what it means to leave our planet a better place than it was when we each arrived here. That is why you have come."

Dr. Dennis Merritt Jones, Bestselling Author of
The Art of Abundance: Ten Rules for a Prosperous Life
www.DennisMerrittJones.com

"Life is busy—and the world is in trouble! But I'm only one person. What's a compassionate educator to do? Here's a resource that's concise, relatable, inspiring, and practical and will help you move from isolation and resignation to effective action with timeless strategies like awareness, linking, and systems thinking.

Cultures don't happen by accident; they are the inevitable outcome of the beliefs and values that inform child-rearing and educational practices. What if we don't have to keep doing the same thing over and over again, expecting different results? What if we rediscover the joy of collaboration and learning?

This book and Renee Beth's Living The Potential Network are giving us the way to connect with a global community working across disciplines to liberate the human spirit and turn the tide of the systemic challenges we are now facing."

Marliese Colantuno, Faculty Member,
Institute for Advanced Montessori Studies

"Renee Beth's focus on valuing the wisdom that exists in all students is timely and commendable. Our work at Taylor Protocols, Inc.—to discover and reveal the innate nature of people—begins with students at the age of about 10-11 years.

Renee Beth's heart and mind are working in a complementary fashion to this effort to lift humanity to higher levels of conscious living, and the conscious education of all. We value her as a strong contributor to this shared mission. This book is another strong step toward waking humanity to higher consciousness, which serves the core motivations of all people. Kudos and best of all things to Renee Beth. She is doing her real work in an admirable way.

Lynn E. Taylor, Creator of the Core Values Index™
President & CEO of Taylor Protocols, Inc.

"*Living The Potential* is a wake-up call, a call to action, and a road map for sustainable, meaningful change. As a Master Certified Coach and passionate champion of the empowerment approach of the coaching paradigm, I wholeheartedly celebrate this book as THE global wake-up call for empowering our youth. The coaching philosophy is based on the belief that every human being is capable, creative, and resourceful. Coaches create a safe environment for clients to access their innate wisdom, so they are empowered to call forth their inspired vision, passion, and creativity. Imagine a world where we apply this core belief with our youth! The possibilities for greater good are endless and transformational."

Fran Fisher, Master Certified Coach,
President of FJFisher Coaching and Consulting
Author of *Calling Forth Greatness*

"Renee Beth Poindexter is fiercely determined to evolve the education paradigm of our society and her book *Living The Potential* eloquently proves the point. This very readable book's narrative style leads by example, inspiring a passionate commitment to this vital priority for humanity's future."

Paul O'Brien, Author of *Intuitive Intelligence:
Make Life Changing Decisions with Perfect Timing*

"Our new generation of gifted children is the way forward, and this book is a powerful guide to help us understand and harness the true potential. Renee has found her passion and put it into purpose with this important read."

Shannon Kaiser, Bestselling Author of
The Self-Love Experiment and
International Life Coach

"I am the father of six children who are all creative and active. They each process information by very different means. Some have excelled best with home schooling while others clearly needed the structure of public schooling. Some have needed additional tutoring. Some have struggled with being bored by the classroom approach. I appreciate that in *Living The Potential,* Renee Beth unfolds a comprehensive approach for individualized learning opportunities. It is thoughtful and effective."

Stephen Cherniske, President of
Altea Health Sciences
Bestselling Author of *The DHEA Breakthrough,*
The Metabolic Plan, and *The Metabolic Makeover*

"I have been a Family Medicine physician for twenty-three years, supporting the health of children of all ages. I have worked at children's summer camps and given health lectures at elementary schools. It is easy to see how the standard sit-in-your-desk-and-listen approach cannot engage everyone or inspire fully, and may not offer a full opportunity for a student to immediately expand on an idea or understanding. *Living The Potential* is not just a book for teachers and parents; it is an important guide to anyone interested in helping others learn."

Natalie Kather, MD, Medical director and
owner of Advanced Family Wellness, Inc.
Co-author of *The Metabolic Makeover*

"Renee Beth's genius is the recognition that we need a new awareness regarding how we educate our children, defining that new awareness, and offering pathways to it. Her discernment of the Earth and all its processes as organic combined with learning as a living process, educes the emergent genius of her students. This emergence will often take the learners to places beyond what anyone could have imagined."

Milton O. Markewitz, Retired from IBM, pro bono
consultant and Vice Chairman of Pull Together Now,
Co-author of *Language of Life: Answers to
Modern Crises in an Ancient Way of Speaking*

"An essential message for our world's future; a call to all of us and our collective responsibility to have our education deliver on its promise—people empowered to share their unique contributions in life."

Anne Adams, PhD, ACS; Integrality.co
Individual, Cultural, and Organizational
Transformation (ICOT Education)

"This book takes the reader on a personal exploration of the frontiers of alternatives to the mainstream of K-12 schooling. Through engaging recollections of her adventure, we are given a glimpse of how Renee Beth has been a pioneer herself and supported the development of several successful alternatives to school. Her experiences of collaborative and humane businesses in health and technology have given her a broad perspective that is well worth adopting. This book is a call for inspiring leadership by relating what it is like to model these examples in not only education, but also in all aspects of society."

Don Berg, Executive Director,
Deeper Learning Advocates
Founder, Attitutor Services
Author of *More Joy More Genius* and
Education Can ONLY Be Offered

Living
The Potential

Engaging the Wisdom of
Our Youth to Save the World

Renee Beth Poindexter

Living The Potential
Engaging the Wisdom of Our Youth to Save the World

Published by
Living The Potential Press
www.livingthepotential.com
Copyright © 2019 *by Renee Beth Poindexter*

Cover Design by Aaron Johnson
Interior Design by Dawn Teagarden

Disclaimer: The Publisher and the Author does not guarantee that anyone following the techniques, suggestions, tips, ideas or strategies will become successful. The advice and strategies contained herein may not be suitable for every situation. The Publisher and Author shall have neither liability nor responsibility to anyone with respect to any loss or damage caused, or alleged to be caused, directly or indirectly by the information in this book. Written permission has been obtained to share the identity of each real individual named in this book.

Any citations or a potential source of information from other organizations or websites given herein does not mean that the Author or Publisher endorses the information/content the website or organization provides or recommendations it may make. It is the readers' responsibility to do their own due diligence when researching information. Also, websites listed or referenced herein may have changed or disappeared from the time that this work was created and the time that it is read.

ISBN: 978-0-9998876-7-7

Printed in the United States of America
www.LivingThePotential.com

To Brent...
One person can make a difference,
and your legacy lives on.

Acknowledgments

TO THE INFINITE and Divine Intelligence that has always been there, patiently holding space for me to slow down enough to receive the treasures that are mine to share and let go of the resistance by deepening my trust in myself and others who resonate.

To My Family...

To my sister Joy, for your compassionate listening. I am filled with gratitude for your support and especially for your awareness to always know exactly what to say at exactly the right time. Your unconditional love has helped more than words can say.

To my husband Mark, for giving me the space I needed to unfold this book. By gifting me private retreats by the ocean, you supported my deep need to BE with nature and mostly in solitude. Sharing your mom and your son, Jesse, and his beautiful family has extended my experience of what family is all about.

To my mom Violet, who made her transition twenty-one years ago. Your belief in me and who I was becoming is with me even today. I will always be grateful for how you allowed me to be your teacher. That role reversal was the beginning of my awareness that wisdom knows no age.

To All of My Past and Present Teachers, Mentors, and Coaches...

To Rhetah Kwan, you have been by my side as a friend and business partner through thick and thin as we have continued to evolve to our next stage of "How do we best serve?" Your loving heart is the gift that keeps on giving and I am forever grateful.

To Carmen, a healer and teacher. Your mentoring has guided me to better self-care for my spirit than I ever could have imagined. Thank you for showing me how to shift my energy through music and dance among so many other tools for becoming bold.

To Joanna, your transformational coaching has awakened a sleeping giant within me. This inner journey continues to deepen and I am so grateful for your guidance.

To Mary Ann, without your capacity to hold the big vision that is coming through me, I would be overwhelmed. Your guiding questions are so essential, including "How do we break this down into baby steps?" I am grateful for you keeping me on track on best practices for lifelong learning.

To Miriam, your wisdom, heart, and expertise is invaluable. Thank you for your participation and always including your invaluable commitment to enlightened leadership.

To My Team...

To Jeremy, your coaching and guidance for building Living the Potential Network is a lifesaver. Your capacity has strengthened how technology can best work for me, rather than the other way around. And to have more fun along the way!

To Fran, your coaching is impeccable; and over the years, your belief in this big vision of mine has never wavered. Thank you for always being there, and for supporting each evolution along the journey.

To Amanda Johnson, my dear friend and writing avatar, who not only knows how to authentically deliver a message from the chrysalis stage to the transformed butterfly, but who has truly lived how to unfold her own potential through many rebirths. Thank you for your wisdom, love, and expertise.

To my co-inspirers, Debbie, Marliese, and Sue, thank you for grounding the Living the Potential Network. Thank you for playing full-out in generating tools, processes, and practices that are life-changing. You reinforce for me how significant it is to be vulnerable, transparent, and courageous.

To My Learning Community...

To Ilana Cameron, you were the inspiration and a co-designer of the Wondertree Learning Center. As one of the first eight-year-olds to show me how to trust my own inner genius and how to have more fun learning, you became the catalyst for this work. Thank you!

To David Marshak, a brilliant mind who furthered Brent Cameron's vision for a holistic learning movement. I have learned more from you than words could ever convey. Thank you for your great generosity and leadership.

To Paul Freedman, your deeply-connected heart and mind are so perfectly aligned for you to lead a revolutionary Master of Arts degree program. And together with our team, we cannot fail!

To Laurel Tien, your commitment to walk your talk as you co-lead our learning community to include diversity with a self-renewing quality is worth more than gold.

To Fleurette Sweeney, your mentorship over the years has fortified my commitment to keep going, and your words continue to reverberate for me: "It's never too late to manifest the dream on my heart." Your belief that it always works out better than one expects, is one of many mantras that I have borrowed long enough to say I own it now.

To my fellow board members, thank you for saying "yes" to bringing yourselves to a big vision that includes your heart and soul. We get to model a much-needed transformational approach to lifelong learning.

To Milt Markewitz, your deep understanding of indigenous wisdom and how we can best wake up to a more harmonious relationship with ourselves, each other, and the Earth we all inhabit continues to be an inspiration for me and so many.

To <u>all</u> of our SelfDesigners, including learners, faculty, and staff. We are being the change we want to see in the world, and it's so worth getting out of our comfort zones to do it. Thank you for your courage and compassion. Without you, this vision would not be built on trusting the seeds of change.

To My Wellness Community...

To Bill Lee, one of the most significant influencers in my life. Your vision is so big that it could also include mine and so many others. I am grateful for how your conscious model of business aligns with bringing the best of nature to humankind, and to you for creating the path for many to bring the best of human nature to our planet Earth.

To Ralph Bietz, for your capacity to mobilize and for showing me how a forward-thinking, for-profit business model can integrate a quadruple bottom line (purpose, people, profit, and planet) and align with a non-profit designed to end world hunger for malnourished children.

To Rhetah Kwan, Renate Lundberg, and Angelyn Toth, for the gifts you have shared with me daily over the past fourteen years. How amazing it is to collaborate with you as we co-generate a living system that continues to attract people who choose to rebuild, repair, and regenerate for today and for future generations.

To Stephen Cherniske, for sharing how energy is the currency of life and how dramatically it impacts everything that I do—and what to do to repair, rebuild, and regenerate on multiple levels and take my awareness to new heights.

To My Readers...

To all of the readers who previewed this book, thank you for your time and your feedback. This book is more true to me and more powerful because of you.

With All My Love and Gratitude,

Renee Beth

Contents

INTRODUCTION
Seeds of Potential

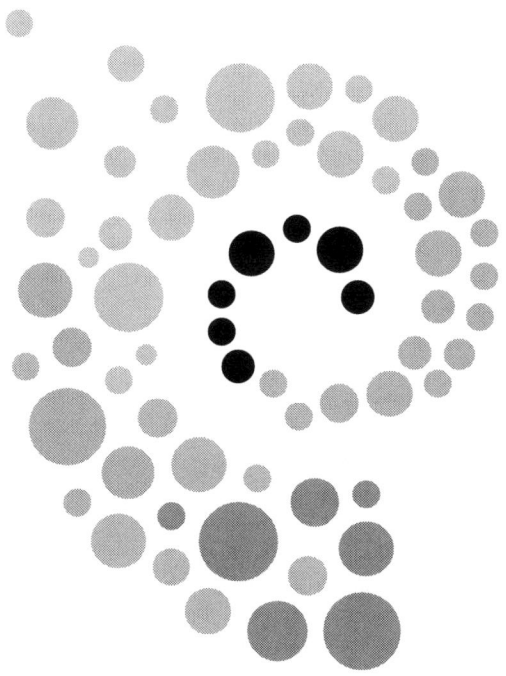

IT WAS SUPPOSED to be a typical morning of project planning with Deborah.

We were a great team and had been working together on a project for a major company that needed to shift their culture from stagnation to innovation. Coffee mugs in hand, we met at the elevator on our way up to our assigned third floor conference room. At the client site, which housed hundreds of cubicles on each floor and buzzed with activity, we preferred this quiet space with white boards on every wall except for the windows that showcased the snowy Mount Hood up against the bright blue cloudless sky. Digging for the root cause issues of this company's problems for weeks, we both realized through our employee interviews that most of the issues this company faced were "people" problems that had begun long before we arrived.

This particular morning, sitting across the large conference room table, I observed Deborah was not her normal chipper self. Normally, this forty-something-year-old woman's green eyes glowed with excitement while we were working; but as she began plugging away at her to-do list, I observed her petite frame hunch forward in her chair and her youthful face scrunch with frustration. Her stature and features usually communicated youthful, kind energy and left people a little stunned when she opened her mouth and let her fierce intelligence and huge visions emerge. But today, she looked to have aged five years overnight.

After we finished catching up on the tasks for the day, I asked her about it with as much lightheartedness as I felt was appropriate. "Hey, what's going on with you today? You look like someone kicked your dog."

Not even a smile, let alone a chuckle. Instead, her jaw clenched.

Oh dear. It must be something serious eating at her.

"Seriously, what's going on?" I closed my notebook to emphasize that I truly was interested in creating a space for her to be heard.

"It happened again, and I am at a loss of what to do." She slumped into the high-back brown leather chair, exasperated.

"Tell me more," I coaxed, leaning forward onto the mahogany table that stretched between us.

"You know my son, Isaac. He just turned thirteen and is really bright and loves learning, but he hates school. Jeff and I have been encouraging him to do his best, but he is so bored. And now he is acting out. We got a call from the principal last night; and because of an incident where he disagreed with a teacher on the cause and impact of climate change, he has been expelled from school." She put her hands over her face in despair.

Oh, my goodness, that's awful. I remember the pain and frustration of being both a student and a teacher that didn't fit the mold. It's so exhausting and infuriating.

I waited quietly for her to continue.

After a few moments, she put her hands back down in her lap and continued, her voice a little shaky. "Both Jeff and I, as entrepreneurs, believe it's important for our son to develop his mind and create meaning based on what's important to him, and yet this critical thinking and self-direction is not always—actually almost never—rewarded in school."

I nodded in agreement. "Have you met with the teacher to seek resolution?"

She shook her head with frustration, sending her stylish sandy brown hairdo into a frenzied dance, and explained, "I've met with the teacher a few times before and totally understand how overwhelmed he is with so many kids and not much time to get all of the material across. He's being pressured to prepare the students for high marks on the standardized tests, and he obviously doesn't really have time to meet the needs of my son."

"I'm sure there is an easier way to support Isaac. Have you thought about homeschooling?" I inquired carefully.

"Not really. Jeff and I both need to dedicate our time to our work. Plus, we aren't teachers and wouldn't know the first thing about helping Isaac learn all that he needs to learn to be successful in this crazy world." A tear slipped down her cheek.

I gave her a moment to breathe.

"What if there was a way, where both you and Jeff could help Isaac see his own true capacity—and both of you as parents could see yours—and then from that, you three could design a learning plan that puts each of you in the driver's seat of your own lifelong learning journey?"

She wiped away the tear and sat upright in her chair. "Sounds interesting. Tell me more."

I explained a little bit about the tool I use to help people of all ages see their unique brilliance and design their learning journeys, and she started to perk up with some hope. In just a few minutes, she was leaning forward, fully engaged, eyes sparkling with hope. Before finishing the conversation, we arranged a time for me to meet Isaac and then also with the three of them as a family.

While Deborah immersed herself back into the project, I turned to look out the window and took a few deep breaths myself.

Something has to be done. If education stays on this course for too much longer, we are going to witness a generation of angry, depressed, and lost people taking over a world that is already in trouble.

Truth be known, I'd already had hundreds of conversations with parents, teachers, entrepreneurs, and learners of all ages about these types of problems. I had seen firsthand what happens when we continue to ignore the fact that something has to change in order to better support people, including our children, in this topsy-turvy world.

What if I'm the one who needs to do something? Hasn't my entire life prepared me to understand where education, business, healthcare, politics, and so many other systems have gone wrong? I do have some answers—but is the world ready to hear what I have to say?

Looking out the window, I got the undeniable intuitive message that I must write a book that shows what's possible when we approach our children and our systems differently.

Experience has shown me that youth like Isaac have answers and solutions to the problems the world is facing. They just need to be surrounded by people and environments that nurture them and facilitate their brilliance. If I could show people what a few elementary school kids accomplished and achieved for the planet when they were approached with a rather large business opportunity, I know it would inspire everyone to consider how we can create environments where children can design their own learning; connect the domains of business, education, health, and technology that have been long-divided; and engage their untapped wisdom to save the world.

I turned from the window back to my desk and started to jot my ideas down.

Yeah, that's it. Living The Potential. That's what's possible.

And with that, my authoring journey began.

The Invitation to See the Truth and Do Something About It

This book is an invitation for us all to take an honest look at our society and begin to wake up to the history we are creating.

Our children are frustrated with a machine-like system that values test scores over learning—and essentially kills the spirit of curiosity in them. Their entrepreneurial parents want to see kids engaged and cringe every time they see their children's creativity crushed. Their teachers are exhausted and unsupported in any effort to go beyond the requirements of the standard core curriculum, as well as heartbroken that they cannot seem to facilitate the outcomes that inspired them to teach in the first place. Businesses are struggling to keep up with innovative ways to reach and delight their customers, and completely baffled by the lack of preparation and skill the new generation is exhibiting in the workplace. And technology is on the verge of being labeled the next addiction of the masses, rather than one of the most phenomenal tools we have to advance our society and our species.

The truth is that our children will not be inheriting a society and lifestyle that you and I have become accustomed to; in fact, they'll live in worse conditions. Unlike the generations that have come before—each one becoming more comfortable and moving up and ahead—this one will face tougher political, economic, and social challenges. And that's just at the collective level. If we look at the statistics around the current mental and emotional health of the individuals in this generation, the future looks very, very bleak.

That is, unless we begin to re-vision the roles we play and bring about the change we want to see for our children and grandchildren.

To upgrade our mechanical, industrial models of education, business, and other domains, it will take a new kind of partnership—one that reflects the organic process of nature.

Think about it, nature *knows* how to grow and evolve. All a seed needs is a fertile environment, some nourishing water, and a little bit of help from some insects to create a plant or tree, which then has the inner technology to continually regenerate and sustain not only itself—but us too.

In the pages of this book, I share an integrative, organic approach to changing this current story; and as you'll see in the subtitle and first chapter of the book, I believe the children are the key to creating a better future and ultimately saving the world.

There is a better way, and the first step in the process is to trust the seeds of change. Trust is the operative word, for without it, we let fear control us. If this fear of change runs us, then we will keep doing what we have always done and continue getting the same diminishing results.

We need to ask the questions that continue to open our peripheral vision, so we have the 360-degree view: Who are we? Where are we going and why? How are we preparing ourselves for this fast-approaching future, and how do we shift the narrative about education, business, and every other domain that is affected by them?

There is a parallel between progressive change in education and change in society toward what a number of people call strong sustainability. For total transformation to occur, there will need to be a shift in education and public awareness, a much closer integration between environmental and economic policy, and a renewal of emphasis on local democracy and activity.

This cannot happen if we do not engage *all* of the stakeholders, including our youth. They have the capacity to tap into naturally inquiring minds, unfold how they are wired to learn, and become leaders for our highest and best outcomes. If you haven't noticed already, our children are wiser than you think, and the stories within these pages may surprise you. And, let's not forget you parents, who hold the power but either don't know you have it or don't know how to use it to accomplish your goals for your children and our world.

But that will all change with this book, as you read about how a small group of young people applied and used technology to manage their learning, and how their teachers and parents became "guides" for the journey. You'll see how they were able to negotiate agreements, design projects, and own their learning experience. By the end of the book, you'll see how the experiences they had in such a remarkable learning environment cultivated a joy of learning and served them well in creating a life of meaning and contribution. They learned who they are as people; they learned how to create meaning; they figured out how to be of service to their community; and most of all, they learned how to unfold and emerge possibilities that weren't there before—and work together and leverage each other's gifts, talents, and experience.

To contrast this experience and show you *why* I am so committed to the message of *Living The Potential*, I am going to give you a glimpse of my own journey. You will see me as a student and teacher who mourned the loss of joy in learning environments; and then watch my adventures as sales director, VP of Sales and Marketing, product manager, regional manager, consultant, coach, mentor, and CEO in my travels through many business sectors, such as construction, technology, software, advertising, financial services, medical equipment and service, and more. My bet is that you will see yourself in one of the settings or plot twists in my story—be it a rough childhood home, an unsupportive classroom environment, a challenging relationship, or one of the offices and conference rooms where I witnessed the absolute disconnection in individuals, organizations, and the domains between them.

It was this disconnection and lack of meaning, which resulted in a serious health crisis, and propelled me into the world of personal development (Total Quality Movement, First Things First, Neuro-Linguistic Programming) and spiritual seeking. Eventually, my journey of getting my own life back on track led me to deep personal inquiries about my role in helping the world to do the same. After several decades of experience in multiple environments, a profound personal awakening, and the experience with these elementary school children, I realized I have the unique ability to connect dots that individuals and groups that were stuck in specialized domains didn't even know existed.

It's taken me some time to figure out how to connect all of these dots in the simplest way possible, but it's finally here and ready for you.

Consider this book an invitation for you to re-engage learning, your children, and the world—and to do so with a sense of clear intention and immediacy.

Whether you are a parent, grandparent, teacher, entrepreneur, corporate executive, or an agent for social, economic, political, or environmental change, my hope is that you will read this book and not only see the solution, but also your particular opportunity to play a part in it. This vision for how we can all work together to live the potential, means we are all in this together. *The* potential is inclusive; it is not mine, or yours, not even **ours**. It is *The Potential,* meaning that we are connected to a living system that includes all of us and all of nature.

My suggestion is that you grab a notebook or journal and keep it nearby while you are reading. I'm sure that you will be inspired with ideas for what's possible for you, for our children, and for our world with this new integrative approach. When you turn the last page, my intention is that you will feel more inspired, optimistic, and equipped to actually be and create the change we need to see in the world.

Together, we can use this more organic approach—trusting the seeds of change, cultivating fertile learning environments, cross-pollinating domains to maximize potential, creating sustainability with regenerative resources, and using the soul of technology to reach upward and beyond—to leave the world much better than we found it.

In fact, my dream is that you will be inspired to join the Living The Potential Network and bring your amazing ideas to collaborate with a network of parents, educators, and business people who are engaging the wisdom of youth to save the world.

Let's do it for the kids, and the kid in all of us.

CHAPTER ONE

Trusting the Seeds of Change

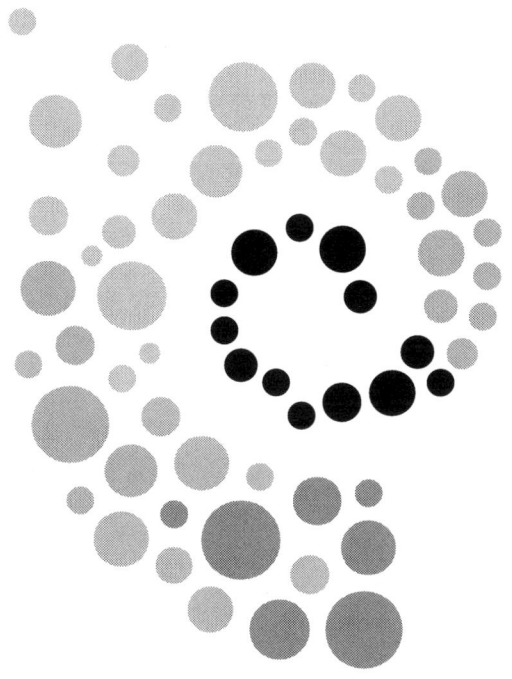

"THEY SAID, 'WE have read about you in the newspaper —that you are using technology to tackle issues facing our communities—and so we thought it makes sense to connect with you. You are the demographic we are looking to reach because we believe you care about the environment, and you can help us design a game that will empower other kids to become energy managers in their homes.'" Brent was leaning forward on his desk.

"Wow. What an opportunity!" I replied, as I bent down to grab my notebook out of my purse.

"Renee," he continued, "imagine corporate managers of a major utility, who oversee electrical power to thousands of households, saying this to a group of students who are of the average age of ten years old, and watching them not even blink an eye with doubt that they could pull it off." He was positively beaming, his eyes dancing with pride.

I smiled back at the thirty-six-year-old founder of Wondertree Learning Center. Brent was an average-looking guy—tall, thin, and balding with dark brown eyes that communicated the depth of his ingenuity. The inspired vision for the learning environment he had created was far from average.

"These corporate players were aware that in order to reach kids, they ought to work with kids, rather than pay the typical consulting group over $200,000 to design a Power Smart game. The concept for this game was that through conservation, the money saved could be placed in savings accounts that would help offset the parent's future education costs for their children, as well as make a positive ecological difference through the smart management of Earth's resources. Isn't that fantastic?" Brent asked, his excitement answering his own question before I could even nod back at him.

"The final negotiation, which was managed by the youth, generated a contract with this major utility, BC Hydro, for $75,000 up front to create the game within the year." His tone was that of a proud papa. "Renee, most people, when I tell them this story, assume that these kids are extremely brilliant, and likely educated at some sort of Ivy League prep school; but the truth is that these kids were disenfranchised from conventional schools, labeled everything from learning disabled to incorrigible to classroom disrupters. The group included children burdened with every learning disability imaginable, straight-A students who found school meaningless, and angry, wild-eyed, rebellious youth. But this innovative learning environment has empowered them by truly listening to them and putting their education back into their hands. And they did it. They didn't just complete the project, they created an excellent product and started a business."

Yes! That's what kids are capable of! They are so full of wisdom and ability—and most parents and teachers have no idea what is contained in the children they interact with every day. But how could they? They're not taught to even look for it, really.

We were sitting in Brent's office in the early hours one morning while the kids worked on their projects in the next room. His office and all of the rooms in the building glowed with the early sunrays that shone through the windows. I looked around, marveling at how this basement of a church had been turned into a bustling learning lab with long tables and chairs, and one especially large round table that could sit twelve chairs comfortably. The top of the table was a colorful mandala, and on my way in, I had observed many of the kids pointing to it as if it were a map helping them discuss their project. There was a section of the room that invited conversations as a living room does with couches, chairs, and even beanbags organized around a rolling blackboard.

As I took in the sights, sounds, and energy of this place, and took notes, I couldn't help but wonder how my life might have turned out differently if I had been nurtured in an environment like this. What might have been possible if someone had seen me—and my strengths—and given me an opportunity like this?

I grew up in the Midwest—Toledo, Ohio, to be exact— the eldest of two children. My dad owned his own construction business and my mother was a stay-at-home-mom until my dad left when I was nine years old. Every once in a while, my dad would come back from California, and we would try to be a normal family, but it never felt quite right.

In fact, sometimes it felt horribly wrong.

One of those weekends he was home, we were at a party and the parents left us kids to play on our own. Four other kids and I thought it would be fun to jump from a picnic table to a clothesline T and then swing like a monkey before falling to the ground. It looked easy enough; but when it was my turn, I missed the clothesline, fell hard to the ground, and broke my arm in four places. I cried hysterically in pain like any child would, but my parents were too busy (or something) to notice. I don't know how I coped with the pain for four days, but that's how long it took them to acknowledge there was a problem and take me to the doctor.

Maybe it's because they thought I was too sensitive.

It's true that I was an old soul in a little body, and I did have very strong feelings about things. It wasn't unusual for me to become extremely emotional while watching my favorite show, *Lassie*. I'd cry my eyes out when that heroic dog would be in a fight for her life, and my parents ultimately forbade me to watch the show without any conversation about my feelings or how to process them.

And then there was that vacation we took as a family, where my dad and I went out on the lake and caught some fish. It was wonderful time with him in the back woods, but when he taught me how to clean the fish and took out the heart while it was still beating, there was no way I could eat that fish for dinner. Sensitive to the energies of nature, I found myself facing overwhelming feelings alone, while my parents appeared baffled and frustrated by my reactions.

My parents were not capable of the awareness that I was a sensitive soul, and it seems most of my teachers were not capable either.

I had several opportunities to experience what they now call "emotional intelligence," but instead of leveraging a teachable moment, they did something else completely.

As a petite five-year-old, wide-eyed, playful little girl, I attended a private Catholic kindergarten run by Sisters who always dressed in their black habits. I remember creating drawings that emanated from the pictures formed in my imagination during a story that was read aloud. Beautiful trees, clouds, the sun, and birds flying along with butterflies. Such a beautiful scene—until I was scolded for not doing it right: "Your flowers do not match the picture in the story" and "You are coloring outside the lines."

My heart sank as I looked around the room and watched other kids receive recognition and praise.

I can't get this right. I can't make them happy. What is wrong with me?

The seeds of not being good enough were planted in my psyche that year, and the big upheaval came when I did not say my lines correctly during the Christmas play. One of the angels gathered around the baby Jesus, I was on the end where I could see my parents in the audience and waved to them before I spoke the lines.

The next day at school, one of the Sisters bent me over and spanked me hard with one of the boards we normally used to build our playhouses for "disrupting the play" with a wave. And of course, she did this in front of all the other children.

My face and body were hot with shame as I got up and walked back to my desk.

I'm not sure exactly when I began to realize that it's not always a good thing to trust the so-called experts, but by the time I got to college and decided to major in English and become a teacher, I was tired of the black-and-white approach to education and students.

It was in my English Literature class that I had my first big run-in with a professor—a short, depressed woman who was hunched over more often than not. With arms crossed, eyes narrowed, and a frown, she regularly displayed her very strong dislike of me and disapproval of my "type"—thin, happy, and involved in campus social activities, such as Rockette, Chi Omega, Little Sister of Minerva SAE fraternity, and more.

I was not the least bit surprised when she gave me a D on a paper I had written about a Robert Frost poem. She had always played favorites in the class, but when I made an appointment to meet with her to inquire why she gave me the D, her feedback stunned me: "I knew Robert Frost personally, and what you have written is not what he would say the poem is about."

Astounded, I looked at her eyeball-to-eyeball, across the desk and said, "Isn't that the whole point of appreciating good literature? Relating to the words in a way that brings forward your own experience, writing about the meaning from a personal point of view, and finding evidence in the piece to back up your interpretation?" I could feel my whole body shaking with resolve.

This experience is singlehandedly responsible for how intentional I became about the quality of education I would deliver as a high school English teacher. I determined to encourage my students to bring forth their own voice and personal self-expression which reflected the message they received from their readings. To create any other environment, I would not be operating from integrity.

Their thoughts, feelings, and opinions matter—and so do mine.

It's no surprise that today, you'll find me regularly talking to parents, teachers, and entrepreneurs about how important it is to bring your inner essence to your life, that real learning is always an inside-out experience, and how unfortunate it is that modern education is about digesting and regurgitating other people's knowledge. How we reflect and choose to assimilate, or not, should be up to each of us as learners.

I know today that my parents and teachers did the best that they knew how, and despite the painful experiences, I am grateful. It was the path to finding and accepting my own purpose—to help children be seen and heard for who they are, not what people want them to be.

The adults who surrounded me in my young life were operating within an old paradigm and model of parenting and educating—one that reflected the industrial model of the times. The conveyor belt moving us from one grade to the next became the linear mechanism that moved small bits of information over many hours (14,000 hours to be exact), forcing external standards to determine the value of the product coming off the line.

Now that we are living in the twenty-first century, it is time to open ourselves up to consider another possibility—something far beyond the industrial paradigm—as this old model is creating more problems than it is solving.

The Wake-up Call

As I write this, America is facing one of its biggest upheavals of the last century, and its population is consequently facing some difficult realities and choices.

We sense the societal change, and it feels out of control; and whether we are aware of it or not, it is impacting our daily reality.

We want the facts, but we've just discovered that many of our news sources are fabricating stories.

We want a change in our government, but our options for candidates leaves much to be desired. And not long after the most recent election, people are wondering if they made the right choice.

We want unlimited amounts of healthcare and not to be denied such care because many are sick with preexisting conditions, and yet we expect that costs should be reduced.

We want the government out of our lives, but revolt at the prospect of any slight cuts to its largest programs like Medicare, Social Security, or the removal of tax benefits for healthcare and home mortgages.

We want better education for our children, but the concept of School Choice fills people with fear of its impact on the existing system and the kids.

And the kids—what's happening with our kids?

It's time to take a hard look at the issues facing our young people today and to recognize that our youth are feeling the stress of life more than the adults around them can understand.

In fact, schools have become center stage for gun violence. Every Town for Gun Safety is an organization that began to track the incidents that have occurred since 2013-2018, and their numbers are alarming. Each year, over 2,700 children and teens are shot and killed, and nearly 14,500 more are shot and injured. An estimated 3 million are exposed to shootings, and our kids and their teachers are now being prepared in emergency drills for what to do when their class-rooms are under siege. It's a trend difficult to face or comprehend.

Why is there so much violence?

Some would say it is because our children are exposed to scenes of bombings, not only in war-torn Syria, but also in shopping malls and concert halls. These images can confuse and frighten kids; and similar to overly violent movies and video games, frequent viewing of news coverage of traumatic events can cause children to become aggressive, desensitized to violence, and less empathetic toward others.

But gun violence is just the tip of the iceberg.

The statistics on bullying alone are mind-boggling. Our children are hurting each other. Every day. At schools. All over the country. In fact, one out of every five students reports being bullied, and it's clear that not all the children are reporting. While school-based bullying prevention programs seem to be helping, too many children are still suffering at the hands of other children who verbally and physically assault them because of their looks, body shape, and race.

Equally upsetting are the statistics of teen substance abuse. Is it boredom? Or is it stress? A feeling of "meaninglessness"? While some teens abuse medicine to party and get high, many are using medicine to manage stress or regulate their lives. Research shows some are abusing prescription stimulants to provide additional energy and increase their ability to focus when they're studying or taking tests. Many young people are abusing pain relievers, tranquilizers, and over-the-counter cough medicine to cope with academic, social, or emotional stress. Most disturbing, two-thirds of teens who report abuse of prescription pain relievers are getting them from friends, family, and acquaintances.

The wild reality here is that teens don't see this behavior as risky. They see their parents taking medicine—and they believe that since medicine is created and tested in a scientific environment, it is therefore safer to use than street drugs, although studies are now showing that nearly 80% of people who inject heroin start by abusing prescription drugs.

And then there are the suicide statistics. Suicide is the *second* leading cause of death for ages 10–24 and for college-age youth and ages 12–18. More teenagers and young adults die from suicide than from cancer, heart disease, AIDS, birth defects, stroke, pneumonia, influenza, and chronic lung disease—*combined.* In fact, each day in our nation, there are an average of over 5,240 attempts by young people grades 7–12.

If our children are our future, these statistics should scare the hell out of us.

Graduation Rates

Some would argue that it's not so bad and point to the fact that graduation rates have been rising since 2002, when the No Child Left Behind Act required states to improve their high school graduation rates. In 2005, the states agreed on a uniform measure of the graduation rate. That meant tracking students all four years in high school.

Since then, the rate improved from 72% to 81% and this rise in national graduation rate was touted by the

Obama administration. But what caused this drastic positive improvement?

National Public Radio Ed conducted research on what was going on, enlisting the help of fourteen reporters at member stations around the country. They identified three major ways that states and districts try to improve their graduation rates by:

1. Stepping in early to keep kids on track.

2. Lowering the bar by offering alternate and easier routes when students falter.

3. Gaming the system by moving likely dropouts off the books by transferring or misclassifying them.

Bottom line, the statistic doesn't tell the whole story. The number is highly subjective or may not be worth the paper it is written on. The high school diploma no longer prepares our kids for a job at a living wage—it's really a stepping-stone for the next level of education.

So, the experts are in a quandary: If they set the bar too high, the students are denied opportunity; if they set it too low, then the diploma becomes devalued. Regardless of what they do, the diploma has virtually lost its value on account of the fact that it only represents a child's ability to regurgitate information on tests. It is no longer a symbol of a child's ability to learn and embody that learning through problem solving and communication.

In other words, the typical American educational experience does not prepare our future leaders for a twenty-first century world that is significantly different than it was even twenty years ago and is constantly changing.

Career Confusion and Chaos

How many people do you know who absolutely despise their job? It seems epidemic because it is. Studies are beginning to show that a large percentage of the population isn't working in the area that they studied and, as a result, they are coming out of college with huge debt and no clear direction of what to do with themselves as a next step to independence.

In a 2014 study, CareerBuilder found that 49% of college graduates had a job that was not related to their major. And according to a November 2013 study by CareerBuilder, about one-third (31%) of college-educated American workers age 35 and older are never employed within their degree field while 51% of employed college graduates were in jobs that did not require a college degree. Interestingly, 90% of graduates felt that college was a worthwhile investment; however, 40% believe that college did not prepare them for the real world.

Regardless of where they find employment, most college graduates have accrued a mountain of debt that needs to be worked off. As of 2013, the Consumer Financial Protection Bureau estimated that outstanding student loan debt in the U.S. was about $1.2 trillion, equal to about $29,000 per student with 18% of college graduates who had a student loan debt of at least $50,000.

In order to pay off that debt, students have to work while many graduates are discovering that the ever-increasing financial burden, combined with the economic recession, have led to a more cut-throat and desperate job market than the one in previous years. It's no wonder that the millennials are thinking twice about going for a degree. If it is not going to help them get where they want to go, why not create an entrepreneurial business and work from home?

Business and Economic Impact

I have been asking this same question of people over my twenty-five years of business development, coaching, and consulting: "How did you choose what you would be doing with your time after you received your education?" Many report that they just fell into their lives, and now they are climbing someone else's ladder, trading hours for dollars and always thinking the grass is greener somewhere else. As a former corporate headhunter and a current business consultant and coach, I have had many conversations with and about people looking for their next best opportunity.

One thing we know for sure: Unfulfilled employees lead to inefficiency, attrition, lower bottom lines, and frustrating cultures in businesses.

Attrition is an indicator that severely impacts the culture of an organization. Average turnover rates vary according to things like discipline/profession, industry, region, and country, and are impacted by factors such as economic conditions, geography and politics, Here's a look at some average U.S. employee turnover rates in 2013, for various industries:

2013 Total Employee Turnover Rate by Industry (U.S.)

All Industries	15.1%
Banking & Finance	17.2%
Healthcare	16.8%
Hospitality	29.3%
Insurance	10.4%
Manufacturing & Distribution	13.3%
Not-for-Profit	15.3%
Services	15.2%
Utilities	7.2%

These are upsetting statistics for these industries because attrition is expensive.

What is a company going to spend in order to compensate for low retention rates? According to a study by the Society for Human Resource Management, employers will need to spend the equivalent of six to nine months of an employee's salary in order to find and train their replacement. Doing the math, that means that for an employee salaried at $60,000, it will cost the company anywhere from $30,000 to $45,000 to hire and train a replacement. Other research shows that the average costs could be even higher. In a study conducted by the Center for America Progress, the cost of losing an employee can be anywhere from 16% of their salary for hourly, unsalaried employees, to 213% of the salary for a highly-trained position. So, when a highly trained executive is making $120,000 a year, and leaves the company, the financial loss could be up to $255,600 to replace.

Attrition also impacts the culture of the company because many departures take an emotional toll on those witnessing them. Watching people go, especially well-liked members of the team, can put a damper on morale. People may be losing more than a colleague— they may be losing a key ally at work and on projects. Others may go through a period of mourning and personal instability. They may start questioning the company, their jobs, and wondering if there are better opportunities elsewhere. Plus, when any employee leaves, the remaining staff and company have to deal with things like redistribution of workloads, instability, and lack of continuity for other stakeholder groups such as customers, suppliers, and partners, and even problems with quality or productivity.

Political Mayhem

It is clear, as we look at the political landscape, that so much has gone awry. Living in the United States, supposedly the most powerful nation in the world, we are having to face up to the fact that some of our elected politicians do not have our best interests at heart. How did we get here?

It is shocking to see that we had a twenty-year low turnout for the national election in 2016. We are one of only a few countries with the highest taxes and no guaranteed health care for our citizens. Our middle class is disappearing, while the elite are being set up to become the ruling class. It appears that campaigns and elections can be bought, so true representation has disappeared. Lobbyists are working hard behind the scenes to bundle their causes into the laws being passed, and our credibility as a country is impacted when our leadership ignores scientific evidence of climate change as a global threat and appears to be creating an "us versus them" fear-based culture.

I believe that all of these issues and more are a wakeup call to mobilize people to fight for democracy —a government for the people by the people.

The system is so broken that it's hard to imagine a way to fix it and restore it to its previous glory.

Rampant Unhappiness

There are deep divisions in our country, not just in income and opportunity but in terms of hopes and dreams. The Brookings Institute reports, "The highest costs of being poor in the U.S. are not in the form of material goods or basic services, as in developing countries, but in the form of unhappiness, stress, and lack of hope."

I think it's safe to say this lack of hope is further shown in the Center of Addictions' report that 90% of all addictions—no matter what the drug—start in the adolescent and young adult years. Unhealthy patterns become lifelong habits, and what is the cost to society in general to be overly medicated and zoned out to the issues facing our society today? Anger management is all the rage (pardon the pun), and why is that? Is it a direct reaction to the symptom we observe as bullying?

Maybe the root cause issue stems from very few opportunities in our daily life (especially in school) to reflect and become aware of the present moment and then choose how to respond to a provocation.

Author of the book *Happiness for All? Unequal Hopes and Lives in Pursuit of the American Dream,* and senior fellow at the Brookings Institute, Carol Graham writes that "individuals with high levels of well-being have better outcomes; they believe in their futures and invest in them." She refers to a study done by David Leonhardt (2015) who found in a Google search that the words of the wealthy—*iPads, foam rollers, and exotic travel destinations*—reflect knowledge acquisition and health-conscious behaviors; yet those of the poor—*guns, video games, diabetes, and fad diets*—reflect desperation, short-term outlooks, and patched-together solutions."

With all of these statistics, I believe that we are facing an epidemic of unhappiness. Bullying, suicide rates, addictions, depression, and all of our cultural and political ills are begging us to pay attention to this unhappiness and find a way to eradicate it from our culture.

The question is: What's fueling the unhappiness?

I believe it has something to do with what we do with these seeds of potential in our children.

Seeds of a New Paradigm

"Wow, Renee, I love your new vision for learning communities. Would you be willing to create an experiential day of learning for our youth (ages 5-15) to show our community a model of enthusiasm for learning?" Her green eyes sparkled with excitement at the idea. She was the board member for one of the churches nearby offering me an amazing opportunity to share my vision with her community.

"Of course! I'd love to!" I gratefully accepted and started brainstorming an experience I could create to demonstrate that learning is an inside-out process to the adults, parents, and grandparents—and show just how fun and engaging it can be at any age.

After some swirls of inspiration, I decided to borrow from *Mork and Mindy*—the sitcom where Mork was from another planet and many times needed Mindy's translation to be understood.

Hmm, maybe I could pull off an ET costume (based on the famous extraterrestrial created by Stephen Spielberg). *Yes, maybe ET could land in this conference with the desire to find out what it's like to be human.*

I started to get excited about creating an interactive play that could engage everyone in the room. At some point, I realized that I would need another character that would be in this with me—someone who could help orchestrate the energy and intention to show the room what's possible when learning is more interactive and playful.

Yes, I'll ask Charles to play God and be ET's translator. I chose my friend Charles McClean (God rest his soul) and he loved the idea.

My plan was simple. Charles would dress in white and sit on a ladder, higher than all of the earthlings. He and I would both have remote controls, so he could translate what the children were saying. Of course, I needed this interpretation because I was from another planet and did not speak the language.

In preparing Charles for his role, I did my best to explain how this *live* play was going to go.

"Okay, this sounds amazing. What are my lines?" he asked enthusiastically.

"Well, Charles, we are going to make this up as we go along. For true learning to occur, we must be *present* to the children, and I'm sure that we will know how to respond and play off of each other as it unfolds. The more we trust ourselves and stay in the moment, the better the experience will be for everyone."

"Oh. Uh. Okay." He was a bit skittish about this approach but willing nonetheless.

I created an interactive space in a hotel breakout room. At the front, we positioned a ladder to create the elevated space where God would sit, and then we arranged five big tables in a large circle where the children would be seated. Each table was filled with activities that would relate to a particular human "sense." Five tables for five senses—sight, smell, taste, feeling, and hearing. Around the perimeter of the room were chairs for the adults.

The expectation was that the children would be the experts on each of these senses, so much so that they would be able to explain to ET what it means to be human.

The parents and teachers in the room did not know the whole plan—only that the kids would be doing arts and crafts at the tables and that I wanted the adults circulating to be supportive of that activity.

When I, as ET, landed in the room with no warning, children and adults were aghast. Some screamed and cried, and many were totally in shock—that is, everyone but "God," who quietly welcomed this far-from-earthly stranger into the room.

I made noises through the remote control and God answered and then spoke to the crowd. "Boys and girls, this is ET, and he says he is on a mission to understand earthlings. Well, he's come to the perfect place because you kids can definitely explain what it means to be human, right?" He went on to introduce the concept of the five senses and how they work to help explain who we are. "So, it's your job to explain the five senses and what it means to be human to ET, using the materials you see on your tables. And don't worry, I'll translate."

The kids interacted with their friends at their tables to get the point across about their particular sense, but they could also come to the rescue of the surrounding tables if they got stuck. After all, they were all on the same mission to explain what it takes to be human.

Each time ET had a question, he used the remote control to share it with God, who would say back to the kids what ET understood or where he needed more clarification.

Time evaporated.

The adults were positively enthralled by what the kids had to say and how empathetic they were to a being that was not like them.

ET had many questions that elicited more and more incredible information from the kids. And when the five senses had been fully explored and demonstrated, ET asked, "Is that it? The five senses? Is that all that makes you earthlings human? I've heard there is another sense called IN-Tu-it? Something like that?"

Suddenly, Timothy, a six-year-old, walked up to ET, took him by the hand, and led him to another table in the center of the room where no one had been sitting. He pointed to the pomegranate that was cut open and all of the red seeds in it and said, "Just like this fruit that has seeds, we have seeds within us that are key to our intuition. And this is the sixth sense."

You could have heard a pin drop in that room. Looking around, I saw adults' mouths agape and children nodding in unison, as if they all knew that what Timothy had said was true.

In the silence, you could hear the same question screaming in every adult's mind: How did this young child have this mature answer at such an early age?

As ET was learning, the adults in the room were learning, too. In fact, they were having a big epiphany: Our children are wiser than we think.

Eventually, the children said they wanted to share the seeds and acorns found on the middle table and took them back to their tables and designed pictures and stories about how human nature and nature are related and connected.

ET began to circulate and learn even more what it means to be human, as he was accepted and no longer feared.

The feeling of love, community, and acceptance of diversity—in all its forms—and the understanding that wisdom knows no age, expanded in the room.

I felt such a deep appreciation for the opportunity to facilitate and experience this moment—to share what I had found to be true: These children—they come with wisdom—and it is our job as mentors, parents, and teachers to see them, hear them, and learn from them. To reflect back to them all of those seeds of genius and possibility that they have to give to the world.

The children in that room were definitely confident with their natural intelligence, not for the typical reasons of having to prove anything, but more for their innate shining brilliance—the kind that is so illuminating that it sparked our adult hearts and minds to begin to take notice: What if the children already have the answers for our evolving consciousness?

The Seeds of a Solution

So, what would happen to the statistics we've seen here if we released the industrial model of education and, in turn, approached our children and their learning environments with this inquiry: What if they have the seeds of wisdom, genius, and possibility already inside of them and our job is to help them uncover those seeds and nurture them, so they can enjoy a meaningful life of contribution?

If children felt valuable, because people in their lives thought they were special and helped them to see all of the other children as special, too:

Would they be as inclined to focus on the differences, make other children feel small, or be defensive, aggressive, or violent?

Would they reach for alcohol and drugs if they spent their time focused on nurturing the seeds of greatness within themselves?

Would they skip out on classes if their teacher really saw them, heard them, and enjoyed witnessing their seeds grow—if they felt like it was an experience that would help them achieve their goals?

Would they enroll in a higher education experience and haphazardly choose classes (and accumulate a bunch of student debt), or would they intentionally design their experience to help them nurture those seeds so they could contribute to society in a meaningful way and make good money?

Would they find themselves in jobs that didn't leverage their seeds of greatness, or would they only say "yes" to positions where the vision of the company aligned with their personal mission and they knew they had the skills?

Would companies experience the same attrition rate if their employees were loving their work?

Would the world struggle for solutions if we had young innovative entrepreneurs creating new solutions?

Would we still be struggling with government, or would we see a new, more mindful and intentional generation rise up to meet its challenges?

Based on my decades of experience in education and business, I can tell you that I know for certain that the change we seek *has* to begin with us—and that it will accelerate when we take some good long looks at ourselves, our colleagues, and our children to uncover and nurture the seeds of genius that are within us all.

How do we do that? Well, a few years ago, I found a tool that makes it a lot easier.

The Core Value Index

Can you imagine a world where you are recognized and rewarded for being your highest and best self—where you have the confidence to bring forth this authentic "being" to the world of "doing" without having to prove that you have what it takes to be successful in the world? Would that offer a more joy-filled experience of life?

When I discovered Taylor Protocols' Core Value Index, I thought, *Finally! There is a tool that can help people understand their internal "wiring"!*

This understanding of a person's innate core nature is the golden key that truly reveals that we have *who* we are to work with, so let's bring *that* to our life, rather than assume we are empty and need to be "filled up" with information to succeed. With the "who," we can unfold the "what" through our natural curiosity and design "how" we want to learn to bring forth our unique essence and create a livelihood. Then, as we pursue knowledge, we can naturally integrate *who* we are with *what* and *how* we are learning—ultimately becoming our highest and best self and unfolding our highest and best work.

In his time, Abraham Maslow was unique in his philosophy as a psychologist. His focus was not to study mental illness but to discover what constitutes positive mental health. He created a model of human beings' needs, arranged like a ladder, with the most basic needs at the bottom focused on the physical: air, water, food, sex. Then came safety needs: security and stability. Then there were the psychological or social needs for belonging, love, and acceptance. At the top were the self-actualizing needs—the need to fulfill oneself and to become all that one is capable of becoming.

Maslow discovered through his research that self-actualized people tend to focus on problems outside of themselves, have a clear sense of what is true and phony, are spontaneous and creative, and are not too bound by social conventions.

Sounds like a great antidote to the ails of our society, doesn't it?

That's why I love the Core Value Index. It provides a process to connect our awareness to our recipe for uniqueness. This revelation enables individuals to bring all of themselves to their learning and their life design. We actually are a human operating system, and we have an internal code—a type of software—that when we work with it instead of against it unconsciously, we activate our gifts and talents, which drive an amazing sense of fulfillment.

Even the quality of our relationships is enhanced. Transformation happens when people not only understand their own core wiring, but also understand that others have their own unique wiring that impacts their way of being. I have witnessed culture shifts in families that begin to understand how each child is unique and different from their parents in how they learn, grow, and develop as human beings; in school environments where teachers are empowered to facilitate dynamic learning environments; and, in businesses that tap into the genius of each person in ways that increase capacity, especially by hiring and placing people into the right positions with greater predictability of success.

Learning how we are wired to learn and lead for our greatest success is a breakthrough that is nothing short of life-changing.

Recently, I worked with a very successful woman from the high-tech industry who has all the trappings of success, but was miserable when we first chatted. She had difficulty sleeping and experienced terrible anxiety on a daily basis. With the results of her Core Value Index, she began to see how she had been warping her core essence in ways that had prevented her from being true to herself. For example, for most of her life, she had motivated herself to be the lone ranger with words like "I can do it myself" and was frequently overwhelmed. Her desire to make a big difference and give back is a dream on her heart, and yet she had been struggling with how to make it happen. When she learned that her core value was Love catalyzed by Truth, and that her core energies were best actualized as a team leader sharing her vision with others, it freed her up to let go of going it alone. Looking inside herself in this way revealed many other possibilities that are now bringing more joy to her life.

When I asked her, "How would your life have been different had you known this about yourself when you were younger?" she quickly answered, "I would have been truer to myself with my choices, and been more confident in bringing my voice and my purpose forward. I would have saved myself a lot of angst about 'fitting' the mold of success as defined by someone else."

I think she's right, not just for her, but for all of us —and especially our children.

CHAPTER TWO
Cultivating Fertile Learning Environments

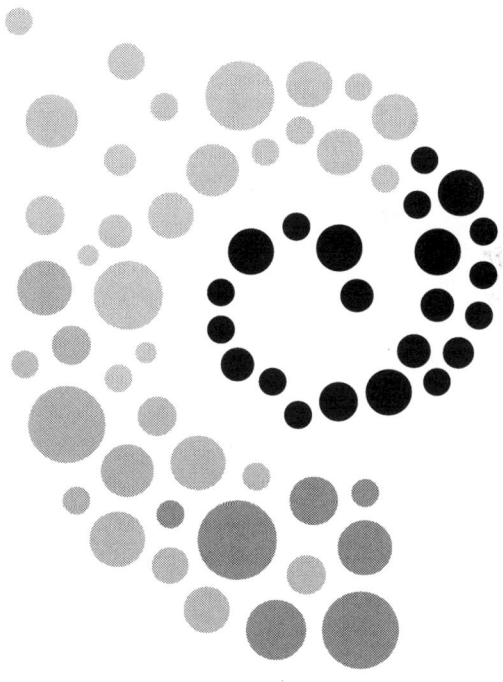

BRENT REFILLED OUR coffee cups as he continued with his story, "With their contract signed and $75,000 in the bank, the kids went to work. They immediately developed a strategy to complete the project and divided up the roles and responsibilities based on individual strengths and interests. There were only two roles they outsourced—a project manager and an expert in programming."

"That's amazing," I responded, eager for him to continue.

"Yes, it was. Their plan to create a virtual reality environment where Robin, the main character, would highlight and demonstrate how each of their major appliances worked in the home, what it would take to make them work more efficiently, and the cost savings that the more efficient approach would generate. There was research to do to fully understand electricity and the electric systems—from the grid to the home and from nature to the grid—and how all of the household appliances work to deliver conveniences we all take for granted."

Wow. Sounds like a very complex project, I thought to myself as he took a sip of his coffee and then set the steaming cup back on the desk between us.

"This meant delving into the deep science of electro fields and all of the algebra and calculus required to understand the conversion of volts, amps, and ohms to units that show up on our electric bills, and then finding the cost savings that one can take to the bank. They even went so far as to discuss the financial possibilities of the monthly savings being invested properly for their future college funds, and how to negotiate with their parents to let them become the energy managers of their households. This led to a 'How to Negotiate' manual." He smiled to himself, obviously relishing the memory of this particular part of the project.

"The artists on the team designed all of the characters, appliances, and illustrations for each screen to capture the attention of their future users, as well as a clickable object that would offer a larger view of what was going on within each element of the various appliances. This led to designing a comic-style coloring book that would be a hands-on tool to match what was happening in the virtual space. As you can see, the project had many moving components and required high levels of learning and mastery of the concepts they intended to teach through the video game."

I nodded at him, a little stunned as I acknowledged the extent of the mastery they had demonstrated. "Yes, they were essentially learning and executing a high school or even college-level project."

I'd known for a long time that kids were capable of more than what they were asked to do in traditional classrooms, but this story was pushing me to think even bigger.

"The best part was the kids' enthusiasm. They were on a quest to discover possibilities and communicate, and they had to engage every subject—art, language, science, geography, technology, and mathematics—to do it. Each day, in their morning project management meetings, the team leaders would update each other on progress and any change orders needed to align the work. Mentors observed regularly how out of chaos emerged stunning solutions. The kids took on the challenges and worked out solutions; and if anyone got stuck in their job, others would make suggestions to create a new way. Everyone could feel the co-ownership of the reality that what they were creating would make a difference, and that they were a team figuring it out as they went." He paused, probably because he saw how wide my eyes were and gave me a second to let it all sink in.

"I wish I'd been here to see this, Brent."

"It was something to witness. Just like real-world entrepreneurs, their very own game design was becoming a real product called The PowerSmart Game, and it would be distributed to all of the seventh and eighth grade classrooms in British Columbia when completed. They were disrupting the typical schooling, and it was fun for them to create a product that would be a catalyst for others to experience it too. All of the stakeholders felt that this game creation was much more than what it appeared to be; and with what they could see in the day to day, it was an awesome learning collaboration to accomplish something that could never have been done by any one of them alone."

Oh, how I wish my students could have had an experience like this!

Brent glanced at the clock. "Renee, I'm going to have to finish this story with you tomorrow. I've got a meeting to attend in a few minutes." He smiled, knowing that the anticipation was going to stay with me through the evening. "Tomorrow?"

"Yes, I'm looking forward to it!" I smiled, grabbed my purse, and left Brent to prepare for his meeting.

As I drove home, I thought about my experiences as a teacher and how hard it was to create powerful learning experiences in a system that wasn't set up to cultivate real learning.

Twelve years earlier, I was a high school English teacher in Ohio. It was a state-of-the-art school in a thriving suburbia where the kids wore shoes I couldn't afford, and the latest architecture offered an open school environment with movable walls for team teaching.

I was committed to helping my students realize that their voice mattered, and I was guiding them into a love of literature and writing as avenues for their expression.

I was responsible for 180 students in six classes covering four different subjects, plus I was a drill team advisor, senior class advisor, and newspaper advisor. Oh, and a drama coach. I suppose it shouldn't have been a surprise that I experienced burnout after six years and had to walk away.

I loved the kids but the system—the culture—was just so out of alignment with my values. I mean, the way they labeled the kids before they even got to my classroom was heartbreaking.

Students had been organized into one of three categories: Adjusted (kids with learning disabilities and low test scores), Normal (kids with average test scores), and then Advanced (the high ACT and IQ kids).

I knew that these measurements were not true indicators of who these students really were, so I let them know up front that we were creating a different kind of environment in our classroom—where they could be their best selves—and that I trusted that they could find meaning in their learning through open discussion and personal reflection. The fact that I cared more about the process of learning than the curriculum itself put me in an interesting conundrum. In open registration, my classes filled up first because the kids loved my class; and as a result, I was shunned by the other teachers, who didn't see the need in having positive connections with their students.

This isolation, the intense workload, and the reality of working in a system that did not make it easy for me to cultivate learning made me feel like no matter how much time I gave to delivering on my commitments, it wasn't enough. When I began to experience serious health issues and went through a challenging divorce, I decided to listen to my intuition and leave the environment altogether.

When I announced I would not be returning the following year, letters from parents flooded my inbox and my kids threw me a surprise "going away" party. I felt so torn, but it was time to take care of myself.

I had no idea that I was actually embarking on a new adventure that would lead to me finding a better way to help children and adults discover and express their potential.

As I pulled into my driveway, I thought, *Maybe someday, I'll be able to bring what Wondertree is doing to the mainstream. It just makes so much more sense.*

It had become so obvious *why* this outdated education system was failing our children.

Limitless Potential vs. Blank or Fixed Slate

First, as I discussed in the first chapter, the outdated system approaches our children as blank slates and empty vessels that need to be filled up with information. Yes, they develop the basic skills of reading, writing, and mathematics, but even that is seen as skill development that needs to be *taught* rather than *cultivated.* Every single child is born with an essence, a purpose, an innate wiring for particular talents, skills, and abilities; but if we don't see those because we're not looking, then the only alternative we have is to assume that they are blank and need to be filled up with whatever information and skills society currently feels is important. Thus, the predominant unconscious assumption today is that we are born into this world empty, and we need to stuff ourselves with knowledge in order to become successful later.

Another pre-dominant assumption is based on the current interpretation of fixed intelligence that is understood to be measured by an IQ test. However, Alfred Binet, the Frenchman from the 1900s who invented the IQ test, did not create it to summarize children's unchangeable intelligence. His goal was to identify children who were not benefitting from the Paris public schools so that new educational programs could be designed to get them back on track. Yet today, our system tends to subscribe to the idea that intelligence is fixed or capped in some way. This is seen in the labeling that occurs with words like "Adjusted, Normal, and Advanced"—that narrows the options and possibilities of each child instead of indicating what methods and practices could cultivate fundamental changes in Intelligence.

What if our ideas about intelligence, and our educational environments, are based on erroneous thinking?

The good news is that with the latest neuro-scientific research now revealing how the brain works, there may be hope for an upgrade in how the experts view schooling and educating our children.

James Gupta, CEO and Founder of Synap—an upcoming education platform that uses research from neuroscience to enhance student learning—explains how science is showing us that the brain is more like a muscle that changes and gets stronger when you use it. "The average human brain has something near 100 BILLION neurons; however, what's truly amazing is that each neuron can connect to up to 10,000 other neurons. That means that we potentially have 100,000,000,000,000, or 100 TRILLION synapses in our brain."

According to David Sousa, author of *How the Brain Learns*, "Learners are more likely to gain greater understanding and derive pleasure from learning when allowed to transform the learning into creative thoughts and projects." The power of transferring learning concepts into practical application during the learning process is that students are able to move through higher levels of complexity of thought. When the brain, operating like a muscle, is exercised the brain grows stronger. According to Sousa's research, when endorphins are released to the brain, they produce a sense of euphoria and stimulate the frontal lobes, which occurs when learners are in a positive environment. This, of course, makes the learning experience more memorable. He reiterates that the opposite is true: If learners are stressed and have a negative feeling about the learning environment, true learning is not likely to occur or be remembered. According to his research, "Cortisol, a hormone that travels through the brain and the body causes a fight or flight frontal lobe activity which is then reduced to centering on the cause of the stress and how to deal with it." He refers to other research that has shown that cortisol tends to interfere with emotional memories, namely that done by Kuhlmann, Kirschbaum, and Wolf in 2005 and Tollenaur, Elzinga, Spinhoven, and Evcracrd in 2009.

We also need to keep in mind that teaching for retention is quite different than teaching for the testing. By re-visiting the information and observing it in different ways, we are creating new connections between existing brain cells.

The learner can grow conceptual frameworks that have meaning and make sense to eventually discover a pattern that connects for the long-term network.

In her book *Mindset: The New Psychology of Success,* Carol Dweck, PhD, reinforces that intelligence is not a fixed quantity, and that scientists have been able to show how the brain grows and gets stronger when we learn. She developed a program called Brainology, where learners discover what happens to the brain when they learn. As Carol describes the program's storyline, "the animated characters Chris and Dahlia, seventh graders who are 'cool' but having problems with their schoolwork, visit the lab of a mad scientist who teaches them all about the brain and the care and feeding of it." Students really enjoy this because it's interactive and they do brain experiments, study videos with real students, and observe how they develop learning strategies. Cultivating this growth mindset, they share an empowering message: "You're in charge of your mind. You can help it grow by using it the right way."

As I shared in chapter one, I think it's clear that we are paying a high price as parents, educators, business people, and citizens for not acknowledging each learner's core wiring, and considering how the human brain works.

What if children were taught that they had innate intelligence and wiring and were given the tools to access and enhance it? I'll tell you what would happen: They would take on and pull off projects like the kids at Wondertree did.

Problem/Solution Project vs. Information Regurgitation

The Wondertree kids were presented with a problem: "How can we teach children and families about energy conservation in a fun and simple way?" And, more importantly, within the presentation of the problem, there was an assumption that they could figure out the solution. This process is real, or rather real world. Learning is connected to solving problems and generating new solutions; it is not about sitting in class all day and receiving, reciting, and regurgitating information that has no direct connection to our lives.

In regular classrooms, too much effort is placed on knowing the answers before we are clear about the questions. The answers become more important than the process of asking questions and solving problems, which is quite possibly the most necessary life skill. Not knowing the answer to well-formed inquiries opens a discovery process, a need to know, which ignites personal engagement and multiple levels of learning.

It's not hard to see the impact of this lack of critical thinking on our society. Young people feel like failures when they don't immediately have an answer, which affects their enthusiasm for learning and creating. Businesses are talking about their difficulty finding young people who can think on their feet. Our political structures are affected because these young people are receiving and operating off of information, without verifying or thinking it through before voting. We are living in a culture where the majority of people mindlessly receive, recite, regurgitate, and act upon information, which is pretty darn scary when you think about the amount of control that gives the media and those who manipulate it.

Curiosity and Strengths vs. Fitting the Mold

Once they were presented with the problem and created a solution, the Wondertree students delegated the roles and activities according to strengths and interests. The natural artists were responsible for the design elements; those who loved science studied electricity; those who were great with math figured out how to make the conversions and show the financial savings attached to conservation; and those adept with relationships and communication took on the tasks of teaching negotiation. Children are naturally wired to be curious. Parents of toddlers will tell you it's impossible to count the amount of times their kids ask, "Why?" every day. What most of them don't know is that these "why" questions begin to unveil clues to the gifts and talent that their children will be bringing forth over time.

Reflect on your own childhood for a moment. What did you use to play with? Where did your imagination take you? And how does any of the playtime relate to who you are and what you do today? The clues were there, but not really present if no one was looking "to see and nurture" them.

When there is a desire to investigate an issue that is relevant to one's interests and strengths, passion is present and fuels the desire to uncover the facts, do the research, test the hypothesis, and ultimately solve the problem. This is a far cry from a system that rewards those who figure out how to play the game of school, pass the tests, get the grades, and fit the mold of a "good student." Those kids rarely get to connect with their interests and curiosity, and over time, they lose touch with them and find themselves in careers and relationships that don't match who they really are.

Collaboration vs. Competition

The kids at Wondertree collaborated with each other to create solutions, to work through challenges as they emerged, and to help each other when one felt stuck. Being part of a project team—working cooperatively, collaborating, engaging, and accepting failure as a part of the process—is all part of real-world learning.

Can you remember the group projects you had to do in school? In my experience, most of them were composed of one or two really advanced kids doing most of the work while the others were carried into a good grade. Eventually, this approach creates a feeling of competition and resentment in a classroom, while some kids work hard for the grade and others skate by. Learning in isolation, kids find themselves competing with the other brains, which ends up fueling a competitive environment and society. It feeds the scarcity and isolation of our workplaces and culture when we are not encouraged to learn how to work together to create solutions. Plus, we miss out on one of the most fulfilling aspects of being human: pleasure shared is doubled. Cognitive development is important, but it cannot be separate from unleashing our emotional intelligence.

Integration vs. Disconnection of Domains

For this project, the kids had to work with many subject matters at once: art/design and its psychology, science, math, finances, verbal and written communication. They had to address all of these at once to create, execute, and evaluate the plan and their progress as a team over time. Again, a far cry from the regular education system where one single subject is taught at a time, and connections are not usually made with other subject areas. Math and science may or may not converse; language and history are not connected; music is not seen as a core subject; sociology and psychology are separate; and with absolutely no prompts for self-reflection and integration, it's really up to the students to figure out how to connect the dots between these subjects.

While it's not real life to think about focusing on only one aspect of a total solution and expecting to get somewhere, this is how our education and businesses and industries are set up. And, I believe it's why there are such huge problems in these systems. Everyone has specialized knowledge, and there are very few people who can speak the language of all the subjects and guide the whole to solutions that work for everyone. I've got more to say about this in chapter three.

Ownership vs. Entitlement

These kids designed, owned, and managed their own learning process. There was no need for classroom motivation or management techniques. There were no promises of good grades or gold stars. They were on a mission, and they stuck to it. They owned it. They managed their learning environment well. How different than regular classrooms, where kids are not given much opportunity to be self-expressed or trusted or encouraged to engage in solving the issues impacting their world today.

Without the core principle of trust in oneself, and in others (including the adults who are themselves conflicted about their role), it becomes a power struggle and sets up a culture of "us versus them." For most kids, there is very little room for personal choice, and this builds resentment leading to rebellion: "You can make me sit down in this seat, but you can't make me pay attention," or, "I am entitled to a better grade because I jumped through all your hoops and that's the least you can do for me."

Facilitating vs. Teaching

One of the things I love most about the approach at Wondertree was the role of the teachers/mentors. They weren't teachers standing in front of the room, disseminating information all day every day. They were sitting around the table with the kids, asking questions, offering suggestions, guiding them when they needed it, and holding the space for the learning that was unfolding. Observing them, I was struck by how vibrant and happy they looked while spending time with the students.

The amount of pressures on teachers in the regular education system today leads to early burnout and disturbing disconnection in the classroom. They are made to focus on teaching information, testing, and managing disruptive behaviors because the kids aren't getting what they need; and their initial dreams of connecting with the hearts and minds of children and making a difference fall to the wayside. Eight hours of disconnected interaction and very strange power dynamics all day is bound to impact a teacher's ability to help the children, as well as the child's ability to connect with authority figures and mentors over time. Hence, it's not difficult to see how this disconnection inevitably impacts their ability to interact with bosses, colleagues, and employees and eventually their own children.

Meaning vs. Obligation

I think the most powerful lesson of the Wondertree story is that these kids were working on a project that was meaningful to them. They saw how important the project was, not only to the conservation of the environment, but to their parents' financial well-being and even their future ability to pay for college. There were multiple levels of meaning that compelled them to take on the project and propelled them forward when it was challenging.

Most children are told what to learn and when to learn it. They are made to follow a production schedule that has no room for personal reflection. They have to prove they are good enough to meet some artificial set of standards, which happens to separate them from their curiosity, strengths, and interests. Where is meaning for these kids who are corralled into regular classrooms? What compels them to learn? What propels them forward when it gets a little challenging? Why aren't we giving these children projects that mean something to them, their families, and their community? Why aren't we cultivating their understanding and experience of being part of something bigger than themselves?

I know there are a lot of heart-centered teachers and administrators in our school systems, and I know they are doing their best. I also know that things are beginning to shift for the better. With the introduction of personalized learning programs, social-emotional intelligence, and the latest trend of mindfulness filling their professional development agendas, I am feeling more optimistic than ever that things are going in a good direction and that teachers will eventually be able to enjoy the work they were called to do.

And here, I think it's really important that we discuss the ones that have the most power to make that change—the parents.

Since the industrial revolution, parents have been encouraged and then mandated to send their children to school. They were assured that experts were going to teach their children what they needed to know to be good, successful citizens. And so, they sent them. For several decades, it seemed this approach to education was churning out good citizens; but times have changed, consciousness has evolved, and the education system is lagging behind.

I can tell you that this mindset of outsourcing the development of our youth is still prevalent among the majority of parents, not because they don't care, but because most of them have no idea that anything else is necessary or possible. Most of them don't know that self-designed learning environments like Wondertree exist, and many of them who have heard about these learning communities are uncertain about taking this new pathway. Will their child *get* everything they need to succeed?

What if we begin now, once and for all, to shift our thinking to the possibility that children are full of potential with the inner wiring to make connections through their own discovery and that the best learning environments are those that nurture their essence, cultivate their problem-solving skills, and give them the opportunity to collaborate and succeed alongside others?

What was your education like? Did you have the opportunity to work on meaningful projects that made you feel like you were part of something important for the world? Did you own your learning process? Were you in an environment that nurtured your innate curiosity and strengths? Were you a people pleaser? Or did you question and retaliate with your opinions with those who had authority over you? Maybe you learned to play the game, and slowly dull your imagination in order to make the grade of what was expected from you. Maybe you didn't see how you were conditioned or groomed to be during these developmental years, and how it set the tone for how you engage at work and at home.

For myself, I did not get to the root cause of my disappointments in life until I made these inquiries for myself. I never felt that my opinions mattered, so I stuffed them and did not learn how to speak from my own voice until I was in my mid-twenties. And I have met people much older than that who can't quite put their finger on what was missing because everyone around them went through the same experience.

That's just the way it is, right?

My answer is **"No."** I can no longer accept this lie we have been telling ourselves. It's time to look with new eyes and accept that we have arrived just in time to co-generate an evolutionary step toward freeing our capacity as humans—listening to the emerging future leaders who are eager to be invited into sharing their authentic selves, as we all design a better world now.

Imagine what would happen to our schools and society if:

- Children were given meaningful projects—with multiple levels of meaning for themselves, their families, and their communities? Enthusiasm lives in this energy, and the desire to know unleashes so much of the what's next. Without desire, we just go through the motions.

- Children owned their learning process and didn't have to be motivated or pushed along by the adults in their lives? They would develop their character because it would be revealed to them as they would be trusted to get in the driver's seat of their own life. Of course mistakes are made, and that is good, for that is the learning for a life well-lived.

- Teachers could facilitate instead of teach, guide instead of disseminate information, and observe the development curve to align the knowledge accumulation based on their learners' desire to know. They would help them to create meaning, unlocking natural passion and creativity.

More importantly, they would experience real connection and mentoring with the students, which is why they signed up to teach in the first place. Doesn't it make sense to create authentic learning environments, where the freedom to grow one's full potential is natural and joy-filled for the students and the teachers?

- Projects required children to interface with multiple subjects and domains to solve problems, and equipped them to approach their other life problems from multiple angles and perspectives? As in real life, it is the integration of knowledge that serves communication and decision-making, and helps in creating solutions from 360 degrees of awareness.

- We facilitated collaboration instead of competition? Wouldn't this open up a wider range of possibilities and learning that engages people to clearly articulate pros and cons to listeners who all work together to sort through best possible options?

- We allowed kids to follow their natural curiosities and strengths instead of trying to fit them into a mold? Remember, we learn to walk and talk without any formal process, other than through observation. Children also learn to read when they are ready. If they are in an environment where reading is happening, they begin to emulate that and figure it out. And, yet, not many people trust this truth and as a result it impacts our children, putting them instead in a very controlled environment that emphasizes this lack of trust in the innate unfolding.

- We treated them and each other as if we already have some innate essence and blueprint of skills, talents, and interests that are uniquely ours to give the world—and that all learning is just a cultivation of those, so they/we can become the best version of them/ourselves?

I know what would happen because I've seen it happen in every fertile learning environment I've observed and facilitated.

We would see happier and healthier children and young adults, engaged parents, and vibrant teachers. Soon after that, we would see businesses and industries transform through the power of curiosity, collaboration, and connection. And eventually, thriving individuals and organizations would go beyond their personal responsibility and begin to work together to shift the collective economic, political, and social paradigms and systems that need to be re-visioned and re-tooled.

Declaration of Learner's Rights and Responsibilities
(developed by Wondertree students)

1.
As a learner I have the right to allow my own experience and enthusiasm to guide my learning.

2.
As a learner I have the right to choose and direct the nature and conditions of my learning experience. As a learner I am responsible for the results I create.

3.
As a learner I have the right to perfect the skills to be a conscious, self-confident and resourceful individual.

4.
As a learner I have the right to be held in respect. It is my responsibility to hold others in respect.

5.
As a learner I have the right to a nurturing and supportive family and community. My family and community have the right and responsibility to be my primary resource.

6.
As a learner I have the right and responsibility to enter into relationships based on mutual choice, collaborative effort, challenge and mutual gain.

7.

As a learner I have the right to be exposed to a diverse array of ideas, experiences, environments, and possibilities. This exposure is the responsibility of myself, my parents and my mentors.

8.

As a learner I have the right to evaluate my learning according to my own sensibilities. I have the right to request and the responsibility to include the evaluations of my mentors.

9.

As a learner I have the right to co-create decisions that involve and concern me.

10.

As a learner I have the right and responsibility to openly consider and respect the ideas of others, whether or not I accept these ideas.

11.

As a learner I have the right to enter a learning organization which offers, spiritual, intellectual, emotional, and physical support, and operates in an open and inclusive manner.

12.

As a learner I have the right of equal access to resources, information and funding.

CHAPTER THREE
Cross-pollinating Domains

THE NEXT MORNING, Brent sat back in his leather chair and smiled proudly as he finished his story.

"It's been extremely successful, Renee. Not just the approach they took to executing this project, but the game itself has been a hit with the utility company and the children who are using it in the schools. They are in the zone. Even the program manager they hired to guide the game development is stunned." His delighted smile emerged again as he pressed his hands together over his heart. "These kids were able to keep the project on time *and* under budget, even with additional features and value-added tools that would encourage their market (science teachers who could integrate this as part of the Earth science unit and for their seventh and eighth grade students) to use the interactive comic book that would take the concepts in the game to another level. The project manager said this was his first experience working with ten and eleven-year-olds on a business project, and he was blown away by the professional engagement of this young team. They were able to get the right skillsets into the right spots, and as the game's storyboards were laid out, there was a listening for new ideas and a quality of decision making that was certainly uncommon from his experience—with *adults* and *executives*. Word got back to the utility company how well the project was going, and they were pleased to hear the good news."

"That's fantastic, Brent. What a great success for Wondertree and everyone involved in the project." I picked up my cup of coffee and let its warmth soak into my hands while I waited for him to continue.

"Yes, and they're not done, which is why I've asked you to chat with me. You've been doing some amazing work with us at Wondertree, helping us see connections to the bigger picture and how we are the 'change' other schools may emulate, but the kids are ready to become serious entrepreneurs."

"What can I do to help?" I leaned back in my chair, excited to hear the plan and be part of these kids' success.

"Well, they've created a solution that is solving a real problem, and the children using the game love it. The utility organization who suggested the PowerSmart project approached me to discuss the possibility of shopping this software to other utility companies in other regions and making it a turnkey solution for other companies. The concept of partnering with education in each city would really improve the image of the whole industry, and they would be the catalyst of the major message of business and education working smart together to protect, improve, and respect natural resources. So, we took it to the kids, and they've created a company called LearningWare, Inc."

Brent's smile lit up the entire room, and I understood it because my heart nearly burst at the thought of business and education working together.

"They're 12–14 years old, and they're ready to scale a business. I love it. And so what role do I play?"

"Well, the kids are looking for partners—people who can shop the software for them because, well, they believe an adult might be more well-received." He smirked, knowing they were probably right. "Your name came up, of course, because you lived in Los Angeles, have already been part of the learning consultant development programs for Wondertree Expansion, and have the education background and experience in business development and marketing. You're the perfect person to help them."

"Brent, I'd love to do this for them!" I could barely keep myself from jumping up and down with joy at the accomplishment of these kids and the opportunity to support them with my own skillset.

After working through the details of this new opportunity with Brent that morning, I immediately set up a business called MetaSource Network and partnered with LearningWare, Inc. Most would never discover that this was a company owned by junior high students who were passionate about making the world a better place and now making a living doing it, but I was pinching myself—delighted to be such an early adopter in facilitating real-life learning projects where young people had a voice in designing their learning and making a difference in the world.

As I interacted with these students and consulted with the utility companies, I was struck by how well-equipped they were for the experience. They had all of the hard and soft skills they needed to be successful in business—skills that are not taught in regular classrooms, even though they are so needed in every industry.

There were many times when I left meetings with them and drove home thinking about my own beginning in the world of business and how I would have been chewed up and spit out if not for skills I'd acquired to survive a tumultuous childhood and then reach the hearts and minds of children in a classroom.

Leaving the world of education with a promise to someday return, I had entered the world of business.

I wanted to connect with people outside the realm of education and learn how people decided to become whatever role they were playing in life, be it a doctor, general contractor, architect, or rocket scientist. How did they figure it out? How did their education prepare them for the life they were living? What, if anything, did they feel was missing despite all of that education?

Out the gate, I was hired to be the first woman business development person in the builder's supply division for a major corporation. What were my qualifications, you ask? I was a woman from Toledo, Ohio—glass capital of the world and home to their corporate office—in the era of Affirmative Action when more women were being recruited to bring a sense of balance to a workplace dominated by men. It probably also helped that I could communicate well, was attractive, and had a pleasing personality.

For the six years prior, my primary customers had been students who were learning to write, speak, and appreciate literature; and I suddenly found myself in a profession where it doesn't do anyone any favors to be a polished speaker with correct sentence structure. In fact, communication didn't seem to be a priority at all. In the six weeks of training and following internship, no one ever mentioned that I would be calling on disgruntled contractors and lumber yards that had been put on allocation for fiberglass building insulation due to the oil crisis.

What a surprise to be thrown out of places where people accused me of taking a job away from a man, and said they would not be placated or seduced into buying because the company had not been there for them for a full two years.

The training I received for the job was not sufficient for the job I had to do in more ways than that. In order to survive and eventually succeed in that environment, I really had to dig deep into my problem-solving and relationship-building capacities, neither of which had been developed by my schooling. In fact, had it not been for my natural ability to read a situation, confront conflict, and navigate difficult relationships developed during my childhood, I think I would have been in big trouble.

I picked myself up, brushed myself off, and went back into those places. I asked questions and listened to these customers to find out what was really going on. I heard their complaints and wrote down the never-ending questions they'd wanted our company to answer, and I promised to deliver the message to the upper management of the company so we could make amends. I knew I was getting close to the root cause of the problem.

Next, I had to get the company to listen to what our key customers were asking for, or we would lose the business to our competitors. I had to get buy-in from both sides, and I worked humbly and resiliently to plant and grow seeds of trust between my company and my customers.

Despite the fact that I was not the right gender in the eyes of many, I earned their respect. I also affirmed for myself that without relationship, there is no learning, breakthrough, or long-term profit.

I took this learning with me into all of my future business endeavors, and I know it is what made me successful in every industry I've engaged: real estate, financial services, healthcare and wellness products and services, public relations, technology hardware solutions and software, marketing, executive coaching, consulting or executive search, and non-profit-development. My capacity to communicate, listen, build rapport, collaborate, and solve problems immediately engendered trust and relationships that grew into very profitable partnerships.

And yet, I repeat, I learned *none* of this in school— at any level of education—unless you count the "School of Hard Knocks."

With every problem, opportunity, relationship, and challenge, I had to dig deep for my own resources or find a mentor to develop and refine my soft skills to work and succeed within the systems.

As someone who has touched all of these industries, it has become clear to me why The World Economic Forum's "The Future Jobs" report in 2016 identified these Top 10 Skills in 2020.

1. Complex Problem Solving
2. Critical Thinking
3. Creativity
4. People Management
5. Coordinating with Others
6. Emotional Intelligence
7. Judgment and Decision-Making
8. Service Orientation
9. Negotiation
10. Cognitive Flexibility

In my experience, these are the skills that have been required to grow all business and industry in the past and present, so why wouldn't they be necessary for the future? The only difference today are the problems these skills are being applied to solve.

The first two and the last one are the hard skills that tend to be more cognitive-based and utilized individually. Complex problem-solving requires critical thinking—the ability to analyze, synthesize, and strategize—and cognitive flexibility that allows one to navigate multiple concepts simultaneously. And then there's creativity—that inventive, out-of-the-box thinking and willingness to ask the difficult questions. We all know that solutions to problems cannot come from the thinking that created them, so if a business has someone sitting there and nodding their head to be politically correct, the company is in deep trouble.

But look at the rest of the list! These have been described as soft skills that enable someone to interact effectively with other people. Business profitability and culture is absolutely contingent on its leaders' and employees' ability to exercise emotional intelligence as they manage and collaborate with others, and make decisions and negotiations on behalf of and within the company. If there is no desire or drive to serve, you can bet your bottom dollar that the bottom line and morale are going to be affected in day-to-day operations and long-term vision.

Creativity often is crushed when there is no self-awareness among employees—when they don't know their strengths and interests and can't appreciate those of their colleagues. It becomes difficult, if not impossible, to collaborate when people don't speak up and step out to share ideas. Even worse, the dynamic will often default to competition, passive-aggressive games, and martyrdom among those who need to be working together toward a solution and adapting to the challenges they confront together. When people begin to operate as lone rangers, they do not build the relationships necessary both inside and outside of the company to move the ball down the field.

In my work as a business consultant for Fortune 500 companies, I heard many leaders complain about employees doing the minimum and not going the extra mile to accomplish what needed to be done. Of course, entitled employees said, "They don't pay me enough to do this," or "I would rather live in a tent than work in a cubicle."

I quickly realized that instant gratification and "doing just enough to get by" seemed to be the norm because there was no "buy-in" to the company's mission—no ownership of each employee's part in making the vision a reality. Taking responsibility and being accountable is not a given in most businesses, and many human resource departments struggle to design workshops that promote teamwork. This concept feels foreign and impossible in competitive environments where people hesitate to share what they know because then someone else might get that pay raise and confirm their feeling that they are underpaid yet more deserving.

Culture emerges from the quality of relationships that co-create the engagements that occur in transactions. When the culture is toxic, it is usually because people have been put in (and accepted) positions that do not align with their core essence and core values. When someone is not "wired" for the job they are in, it affects how they feel about themselves and their work; and that dissatisfaction affects every interaction they have with management, colleagues, and customers.

It's been proven over and over that a common sense of purpose among leaders and employees is what makes a company's vision come alive. Vibrant vision and mission invigorates individuals to own their part and deliver on the strategic plan and the day-to-day tactical implementation. And it's not something that can be inspired overnight or in a one-day workshop on culture. To see a change, everyone has to own the vision, including those in the c-suite—those who often don't realize that everything they think, say, and do reverberates throughout their organization. They must be the first to own it, emanate it, and reward it as they see it inspired in others.

I believe this is why relationship marketing is so successful. People find a product or service that changes their lives, and they begin to share it with the people they care about. With a decentralized distribution system focused on serving others and rewarding them financially to do it, a natural web of relationships with family and friends is formed. They grow their knowledge through experiential learning and personal development. As a result, they begin to share with their extended family and friends, and before you know it, there is a whole tribe of people feeling better and making good money.

It all comes down to relationships.

Cross-Pollinating Education and Business

I was thrilled when I got the call. One of the largest school districts in the state of California had secured a grant to fund a concept called "Business Solutions in the Classroom," and they were looking for a facilitator to develop the processes and curriculum for this to happen.

A real opportunity to share my grandiose idea of designing real-world learning environments for teens!

I packed my bags and flew to meet with the County Office of Education to sign the contract and begin my initial interviews with the different department heads. In my mind, it was vital to meet the power players of all of the "domains" of knowledge—math, science, language, history, business, etc.— to capture their view on their subject as integral to preparing their students for life beyond the classroom.

As part of my research, I also connected with many of the local businesses surrounding the high schools in that district and interviewed several who had provided internships for the students in the past. Plus, I spent time at the chamber of commerce meetings and a couple of education conferences. It was important for me to hang out in the cafeteria and roam the halls to connect with the students and get a glimpse into their world.

After perusing this terrain of intricate relationships for a few weeks, I felt a deep sense of despair.

Business people were frustrated that the students they had employed over the summer or after school were "useless" and "lazy" and, worse, "not trustworthy!" Many of the teachers were exhausted and overwhelmed with so many behavior issues in the classroom, and beside themselves that they couldn't really get through all of the subject matter they were hired to teach. Overall, the stress was so thick you would need a chainsaw to cut through it all. And then the kids themselves seemed disconnected from why they had to be there at all, except for the social aspects, which encouraged skipping class and acting out to be the center of attention.

With my glass-half-full mindset, I set the intention to bring these factions together in a way that would raise the bar beyond what anyone had expected or could even dream possible.

I know just how to get them to play on the same team. I'm going to facilitate an experience in which all of these stakeholders will take part in real-world scenarios where they have to pull together to make it work or none of them will be successful. All for One. One for All.

I put together a series of exercises that would match projects with project teams, bringing together the right skillsets, regardless of the department, the business, or the grade level. Weaving in the cognitive elements of SWOT analysis—strategic planning, product/program development, marketing, cash flow projections, talent recruitment, retention, and evaluation—all partners would see both the "business of education" and the "education of business."

*It is important to get the leaders on the same page—
to move beyond the "us versus them" that is keeping them
from working on those win-win possibilities. If the guides
can't get there, how in the world can the students—their
customers and future employees or partners—ever feel
safe enough to learn to trust themselves in a perceived
mistake-free zone?*

I knew to be ready for the unexpected and so
sprinkled in emotional intelligence strategies, neuro-
linguistic programing tools, and a good dose of conflict
resolution, mediation, and humor.

Laughter cures all—keep them laughing.

I was filled with anticipation and all set for the
three-day retreat at the mountain. And then I got
the bad news: the selected students would not be in
attendance. At the last minute, it was determined it
would be too much of a liability to have the students
participate in an overnight excursion.

My heart sank.

*I really wanted this breakthrough for the students—
to experience a resourceful community of support that
empowered them to step up and into their own role, and
leave behind the victim mindset. Damn. Well, I'm going
to have to over-deliver for these teachers and business
partners.*

Bringing the teachers and the business partners
together in the same space was my opportunity to
build a sense of relatedness—to join their hearts and
minds together to solve the problem: "How do we, as
stakeholders, create meaningful learning projects that
prepare students for the real world?"

As always, my first step is listening, and I was not surprised by what I heard.

The business partners looked at the teachers and explained, "You're not doing your job. They are not hirable."

The teachers shot back, "If you only knew what was happening in the classroom, then you would understand."

When they had all shared their thoughts and feelings, I stepped in. "Yes, you are both right. These kids are unhappy. You teachers are unhappy. You business partners are unhappy. And you all have *good reason* to be unhappy, and a good reason to participate today and co-create a new possibility. Let's start with the aligned intention to create scenarios where students get real-world experience and are so excited about learning that you teachers' jobs become easier and you business partners find yourself thrilled to hire the students who come out of this process."

The retreat was a thrilling success. With new relationships and a new narrative that they committed to write together, all of the stakeholders finally had the leverage to make a bigger difference together. There was a shift in perspective when a new bridge opened and connected the business people to be a resource for the students as well as the teachers.

The teachers began to experience that they weren't alone in their endeavor to "wake kids up" to what would be expected from them when they entered the world "out there." The scenarios for projects that emerged from the teachers and the business community began to provide the students with real-world problems that businesses in the community needed to have solved; and the students got a taste of the real world for themselves as they took on challenges that others expected they could solve.

For example, a workout facility needed a new marketing campaign. This became a project that took on new energy with the voice of the youth. There was a desire to deliver the best message, and the task required an assimilation of biology, art, health, writing, sociology/psychology, along with various software programs. Collaboration became central to the project's success, and learning was suddenly fun and happened at many levels for the stakeholders who wanted to design real-world learning. As the teachers and business owners came together for the students, they began to experience that they, too, were learners learning about learning with new eyes.

It was win-win-win all around!

The Value of Cross-Pollination

So, imagine, one of these Wondertree kids showing up to *your* workplace, with all of their problem-solving ability and relationships skills. Imagine having their critical-thinking and negotiation skills on the projects that matter most in *your* company. Imagine leveraging their experience in project management and their ability to collaborate and coordinate with others to get *your* company results in a timely manner under budget. Imagine the teams they would lead and guide with their high levels of self-awareness, personal reflection, empathy, respectful communication, and ability to understand and interact with other points of view. Imagine their creativity and possibility-thinking impacting the development and fulfillment of *your* products and services. Imagine the clean, organized communication that would occur in an effort to create win-wins for everyone on the team. Imagine watching them theorize, test, fail, and try again—without all of the drama. But most importantly, imagine the drive and determination that would affect *your* company because they want to make a difference in the world, and have chosen your company's vision and mission to do it.

I know, I know—all of you business owners are thinking about calling me up and asking for these kids' numbers. And I don't blame you one bit. Who do you think I called when it was time for me to launch this message?

But listen. While you may be imagining that these particular kids are the answer to your business's needs, I want you to see that *you* have kids like this waiting for you in your local school districts.

What if you and your company looked at all of the projects you have on the docket and enlisted the creativity and problem-solving abilities of the kids in your local schools? What if you gave them the opportunity to connect with their interests, passions, and strengths and become part of something bigger than themselves? What if you became a catalyst for more children to get this type of experience *before* they end up asking you for a job in ten years?

Should this be such a big leap of faith? Don't we all accept that "kids say the darndest things" and that yes, it is "out of the mouths of babes" that we hear some of the greatest bits of wisdom? If you still find yourself doubting, tune into YouTube and listen to Logan LaPlante speak about hack-schooling—how he has taken charge of his learning through a blend of internships. He is the voice of this generation, trying to help business owners like you and me realize that learning beyond the traditional classroom is necessary in order to experientially integrate learning and create meaningful careers.

We need business to cross-pollinate with and partner with fertile learning environments, and enlist the wisdom of our youth to solve real problems; and we need the education system to be open to that level of interaction.

It would be a revolutionary and evolutionary step to have businesses and community organizations align with teachers to provide projects where students can apply knowledge in ways that reveal what it takes to succeed, how to work with other people to get things done in real time, and why it's important to connect to work that will spark their uniquely meaningful path of contribution to the world.

CHAPTER FOUR

Sustaining with Regenerative Resources and Systems

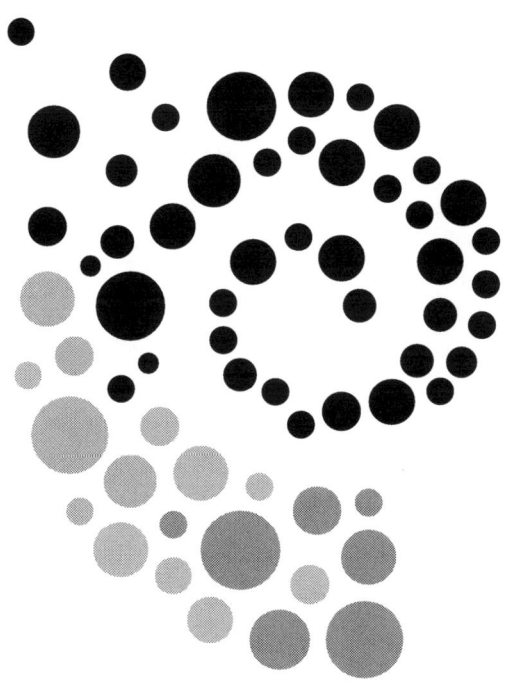

"GUESS WHAT! THERE are two major utility companies in Southern California that are entertaining the concept of the PowerSmart Game, and we are moving forward with next-step discussions." I was so excited that I blurted it the minute I reached Brent's office door.

He leaned back and folded his hands while I settled into the leather chair across from him. "That's terrific, Renee! Which one do you think will land first?"

"I think it will be the municipal district with less bureaucracy. My next meeting with them is Monday. I am working on the presentation to show them the framework design of the game, and then determine how many changes we will need to make it to align with the distinctions of their terrain and regional requirements. The primary subsidiary is still interested, but it looks like they are putting it off 'til next year." I paused, thinking about the last meeting I'd attended. "You know, sometimes I feel like I'm undercover."

"What do you mean?" he asked.

"Well, I am negotiating huge deals with major executives, but I never mention that the corporate executives of Learning Ware, Inc. is a team of junior high students."

He laughed out loud with me. "Well, I'm looking forward to seeing how this all unfolds. Any details you would like to discuss?"

"Yes, a few," I pulled out my legal pad, and we finished hammering out the last of the details.

The project went right along without a hitch, and it was determined that I would also be the facilitator to work with the school district's middle schools' science teachers in the rollout.

I was thrilled to participate at that level and arrived eager to support the teachers in making the game a central component of the unit of study, which is why I was stunned when I was told that it was going to be used as an incentive for the students who got their primary work done first.

What? But this is a fun way to learn all that stuff! I thought to myself.

It was heartbreaking to watch as the students were instructed to copy, word-for-word, the worksheets that were projected from the overhead projector and then take it home to work on the problems. There was no interaction or excitement about what they were learning.

Wow. These teachers have the ability to engage and open the minds and hearts of these students by getting them connected to the virtual reality of Robin's household, starting with the fact that electricity doesn't just happen with the flip of a switch. There's a whole lot goin' on, which would lead to other amazing aha's. I clenched my fists in frustration at the back of the classroom and focused on long deep breaths as I watched the children mindlessly copy down information that didn't inspire or engage them.

I was hopeful that other teachers would be more open to making science come alive, as a fun and inspiring opportunity for the children to share their learning with their parents, which would then create more support for the teachers. At Wondertree, it was understood that a key to learning is the invitation itself: "Why are we doing this, and what difference will it make to the students?" It was obvious to us that when kids connect their education to their lives beyond the classroom, their learning is more engaging and long-lasting.

Unfortunately, these teachers were not allowed to use it as a core approach to study, and they missed out on something that would have brought life and joy back to their classrooms.

Sustainability

Sometimes, great ideas are ahead of their time, and cycles of innovation are tricky when it comes to how long a concept can be sustained. In qualitative research, we know by studying consumers that there are the innovators, early adopters, late majority, and laggards; and we were ready for all of them. What we didn't see coming was all of the governmental legislation of regulation, or deregulation, that would impact our business strategy for LearningWare, Inc.

We started our great idea during the regulation phase, which had created the conservation strategy to help manage the existing power and provide incentives and rebates to people. And it lit up the people who aligned with the "green" environmental movement. Unfortunately, with newly elected officials, the tide turned to deregulation, primarily for the financial reasons to push more power usage and forget the incentives and rebates. So, although we had a great way for business and education to partner on something meaningful, it wasn't auto-renewing or sustainable.

Two years after the kids had begun the project, I sat across from Brent, utterly frustrated.

"Brent, I'm so upset that these kids' brilliant game is impacted by something like this." I looked down at my fingers, trying to keep my frustration from oozing all over the room.

"I know, Renee. It is really frustrating, but it's also the nature of business and life, isn't it? Things change, and these kids are learning that, too. The good news is that even though the business isn't going to continue the way they imagined, they have gained a ton from the experience of creating and launching it. Can you imagine knowing what they know at their age?"

"You're right. They have gained so much, and that learning will stay with them." I looked up and smiled.

It's true. What profound lessons to learn so young.

"Yes, and there are already other projects on the drawing board, as they design the next steps of their portfolio development." Brent's smile and assurance melted away my frustration, and we finished the meeting by discussing my next role in the development of Wondertree.

As I jumped on board to create a future path for Wondertree, I began to ask big questions about sustainability and what is really necessary to create it for our children and our planet.

Over the next few years, I had the opportunity to interact with some businesses and products that helped me form a better picture of how we can more consciously design our learning for an authentic life— one worth living—as well as reflect on what happens when we don't.

Customer Centrism

I spent about nine years in the health care industry and was in the early stages of that journey when I first met Brent. A business development specialist, I marketed high-end medical equipment designed for the cardio-pulmonary divisions of hospitals. This included life support systems and operating room equipment— ventilators, respirators, and liquid oxygen. It was a competitive industry, and I experienced how decisions were made, and how they weren't always made for the right reasons.

Call me naïve, but I was shocked to see doctors seduced by competitors who offered weaker solutions, but gave them keys to a brand new Jaguar. And then I was mortified when this unethical approach earned the large order to supply all of the hospital's ventilators. I came to realize that decisions were not always made for the highest and best good for the people involved, but rather for under-the-radar personal gain. Furthermore, I observed how patients dealing with cancer and cardio-obstructive pulmonary disease lived unaware of how their lifestyle choices impacted their well-being. I will never forget the image of a woman with a trach inserted into a hole in her throat, demanding to have her cigarette, somehow not understanding how she was exasperating her condition.

Realizing this was an unhealthy environment, I decided to leave this job and enter the home health arena where I could help the respiratory therapists and nurses who could more easily educate patients on self-care and assist them into a healthier lifestyle. In this role, my primary responsibility was to develop the business of consistent referrals for our company, so that when the patients returned home from the hospital, all of their durable medical equipment needs would be provided along with the medical services. I had a sales team of ten business development specialists whose primary job was to call on the discharge planners of the hospitals throughout Southern California, and I would develop the contracts for the services rendered and a plan for quality service renewals.

Of course, I didn't know what I didn't know, but I quickly discovered how the system was missing key elements. We were selling a service to the discharge planners—people who did not use the service themselves, since it was for the patients—and also one that they didn't pay for, since all billing occurred through the insurance companies. Again, I felt there was something missing, and it had to do with the lack of quality communication between all of the engaged stakeholders for the sake of getting the patients what they needed. There were many breakdowns in this supply chain, and one in particular stood out for me.

Jane, a seventy-year-old woman was released with chronic pulmonary disease. Her cardiologist had prescribed a nebulizer to support her breathing, along with several other medications. Our company delivered the respiratory equipment, along with the other medical equipment. Jane's condition worsened, and she soon needed more than the weekly visits we were assigned for her care. We communicated this need, but the insurance companies messed up the billing, which created more stress for Jane and exacerbated her condition. As I dug into the cause of the problem, I realized it all could have been solved if the right codes had been used to update her discharge, which required communication between the various departments in the hospital. As it turned out, our home care service was the only consistent support Jane had, and she needed so much more than that. Although electronic medical records are now a part of the solution, separate departments within the hospitals and their vendors are not always on the same page. The patients don't really know this, but the impact is life-threatening, so much so that patient advocacy has now become a profession.

Even though my position was to get the business and keep the business through high-quality reviews, I did not have a strong sense that the operational side of our company was able to deliver on the promises I was making to our hospitals. In order to remedy this, I began to spend time in the operations where I learned that the operations manager was not a systems thinker; thus, the breakdowns were not handled by developing root-cause solutions. Knowing that my sales team and their customers—the discharge planners of the hospital—depended on the quality services our operations would deliver, I continued to work to make the difference needed. But it was hard, and it seemed like there were even more forces working against my efforts. The whole industry of healthcare suddenly found itself in the midst of a paradigm shift—one where the doctors' power position was shifting to the insurance companies, and the pharmaceutical industry merged into what they call Managed Care. I witnessed the doctors losing their influence through this process, and it was like watching a herd of deer in the headlights.

Oh no! Now who will be able to help the patients with their health—with all of these intermediaries in the midst?

It reminded me of how I had seen the students' needs going unheard by the upper echelon.

And then I had my own wake-up call.

Individual Responsibility

After years in this rat race, I was so exhausted that I would come home on Friday and sleep until Monday morning and get up and do it again. That is until my good friend, Megan, did an intervention—rescuing me from a cycle of desperately taking on more than my fair share to make up for the lack of commitment in others. I was somehow unconscious that this way of being was not sustainable, but my body knew better.

Megan introduced me to a homeopathic doctor who quickly determined I had Epstein Barr/Chronic Fatigue and put me on disability for six months. Sleep was my primary objective, and reducing stress was a byproduct. So was learning to just *be* instead of *drive* to *do* to make a difference. It was time for me to re-examine my life, heal, and figure out how to create a new reality. I had to let go of all my already-thinking—*the past programming and automatic default to work myself to death*—and just take each moment as it came, and breathe, and get more connected to myself. Through meditating, journaling, container gardening, and taking walks in nature, I slowly learned how to nourish myself. I saw the power of my mind, my consciousness, and my thoughts; and from this new awareness, I began to create a new possibility for my life.

It was my good fortune to be the patient of a holistic physician who did not become preoccupied with my symptoms but instead treated the root cause of my illness. As a result of sound and light therapies, homeopathic remedies, and a nourishing natural foods diet, I experienced regeneration and moved beyond what the so-called experts thought was possible. It was miraculous, as I trusted that my body has its own capacity to heal when given the right conditions to do so, which included bringing "all" of me—my mind, my body, my heart, and my spirit—and the support of a healer who could give me the time I needed to recover my whole system alignment.

Through this "inside-out" experience, I began to see with new eyes.

There is a natural process for healing, and as I tuned into the biological process, I became aware of how we are all part of a living system—an ecology—that not only connects the inner systems to the outer, but that is interdependent on all of nature. This re-awakened in me the passion I have for people and my desire to be of service to them.

I determined to somehow show others how designing a life is an inside-out process.

How could I leverage my experience and empower others to live with more authenticity as a part of the connected whole? That's when I trusted my inspiration to follow my heart—to re-enter the domain of education armed with the intention of co-developing a learning community that was self-renewing and sustainable, much like what I had experienced with Wondertree.

Sustainable Education

Quickly, I put my condo in Redondo up for sale and prepared to move to Oregon. I was on a mission to design learning environments where the basics of communication were not simply taught as part of a curriculum or unit of study, but would become a foundational principle for flipping the typical schooling paradigm.

The students would be called learners, and the teachers would be honored guides. Natural curiosity would be the driving power that fueled the WHY, which would become the catalyst for the WHAT. As a learning community, we would research and approach the problems we wanted to solve. And, of course, the HOW would be the best approach to accomplish the shared outcome.

The approach was called Enthusiasm for Learning, and I trusted that the learners could actually drive their desire to learn from the inside out. Project-based learning became a key strategy—a framework that was flexible enough to integrate knowledge accumulation from the different subject areas of art, science/math, geography, history, language, sociology, and psychology.

Inspired by the Wondertree model, I worked with two partners; and we were driven by a vision of unleashing natural intelligence in ways that would facilitate learners in unfolding their character. By learning who they were in relation to others, they would also learn how to honor ways of being through their personal reflections. These attributes would be cultivated at an early age, so they would learn how to learn, be empowered to be responsible for results, understand how to work with others and appreciate diversity, and develop a sense of environmental ecology. And all of this would be occurring simultaneously as they each designed their own portfolios.

Timing is everything—and to every thing, there is a season.

In 1995, the Charter School Bill was being introduced as a part of the political process. Not long after I had set up my new home, I found myself presenting alongside other zealots to the Oregon Legislature, advocating for positive changes within our schools. The Charter process allowed for creative innovations, and it was a pathway for public schools to open up to these innovations and provide the tax dollars to the innovators.

It was very exciting. Two of my colleagues and I promoted our vision, and everything was lining up. We had more than sixty interested parents who wanted their teens to participate in our Teen College, and a church that offered their basement location for our classes. It was perfect with a commercial kitchen, a stage, several enclosed offices, and a huge open space. It even had a garden where we could grow our own herbs and vegetables. This was a perfect place to launch as we ultimately were planning on building out a warehouse space that would include all of this and more—one that the learners would help to design and build.

As we continued to show up and bring forth the voices of teachers, parents, teens, we noticed that the legislators were not always present. They were there physically, but their minds were somewhere else. Somehow, we were not connecting with their hearts, and I had a sinking feeling that this bill was not going to pass. It didn't matter how committed we were, we were still dependent upon a political system that was somehow unwilling to respond to the possibility of a new future in which we actually could address many of the root cause problems facing our state.

Sadly, I was right. The Charter School Bill did not pass. (It did eventually pass four years later in 1999.)

After a stint in a local technology company that proved to me again that there was much work to do to bridge education and business (more on that in chapter five), I decided to take a trip to India to see if I could find some clarity about next steps.

Sustainable Finances

George Harrison once said that life happens while you are making other plans, and that's been true for me. While I was in India, my mom passed away; and upon my return, I became the executor of her estate.

In addition to the experience of the grief of losing a parent, I was struck by something even heavier as I reviewed her financials. She did not know how to manage her money, and she had left behind a horrible mess for me to clean up.

Why isn't financial well-being part of education, for heaven's sake? I wondered as I struggled through paperwork and meetings and negotiations on her behalf.

Realizing what a huge problem this lack of financial literacy had created for my mother and several family members and friends, I began my studies to become a financial planner. My goal was to learn all about money and help others to become aware of how money could work for them. The learning curve was steep—getting all of the licenses for insurance and securities—but I was excited to help others.

Once I began this journey as a financial planner, I quickly learned that my agenda was vastly different than the industry's. Again, there were the experts who were set up to manage the money, and then the people who believed they could not do it on their own and needed the experts. The only problem was that these experts were more inclined to sell financial products for fees and commissions than to teach people how to make informed investment decisions on their own. As soon as I saw the game that was being played, I said goodbye to the industry.

I took what I had learned about financial literacy and looked for a better way to share it—a way to help people learn about money and manage it in a way that they could embrace financial security and perhaps uncover the secrets for financial freedom.

Sustainable Health

As I continued along my own journey, deepening my experience in both business and entrepreneurship, I learned how important it is to create multiple streams of income. Then, through my alternative learning with Erickson School of Coaching, and my Neuro-Linguistic Programming Certification, I realized that my business would need to have a well-being component. My own healing journey would never have occurred without the healing crisis that had opened me up to naturopathy and homeopathy, and I wanted others to benefit from more powerful approaches to their health.

In my heart of hearts, I knew that people who knew better would do better.

When it came to finding support for physical well-being, I could see a core problem: The pharmaceutical industry was inundating people with commercials related to drugs that could address the symptoms but not the problem. My goal was to find a conscious company that understood its relationship to nature—that saw itself as part of a self-renewing community of care. And I knew, beyond a shadow of doubt, that in order for a company to have this as part of its cultural mandate, it would first have to be an integral core value of the founder and owner. Many people do not feel business can be altruistic in its vision, but I knew, despite my previous business experience, that there had to be business leaders who had their head and heart connected.

As I continued to read, study, and explore nutritional research and holistic approaches to healing, I was guided to one such company.

In 2004, I was invited by my friend, Rhetah, to visit the headquarters of a holding company called the Econet near Seattle, WA. As soon as I walked into the lobby, I was mesmerized by a huge global map—more like a mural—that took up the space of the entire north wall. When I moved closer, I could see that it was highlighting the company's growing fields that were located in five climate zones as well as the manufacturing facilities, plantations, and other corporate office located in South Korea. On the east wall was a painting of the founder Yun Ho Lee with his son, Bill Lee, kneeling down in an aloe field. I was moved to see how this father had left his legacy with his son who picked up the baton, inspired to commit his own life to "bring the best of nature to humankind."

There is something beautiful here. This just may be the visionary company I have been looking for.

That day, there was a luncheon where several key people from the company told the history of the Econet and the five companies that make up the holding company: Unigen–the scientific research division; Naturetech–the manufacturing arm; Aloe Corp–the agricultural division; Serve First–the non-profit group dedicated to ending world hunger for malnourished children; and, Univera–the distribution arm. After lunch, there was a tour of the genomic science laboratory.

This is impressive. I would love to meet the founder and try these formulas.

Bill Lee had invested over $100 million dollars in research to uncover the healing properties of over 18,000 plants that were dedicated to address the root cause of inflammation, wear and tear, and oxidative stress on the human body. Speaker after speaker shared the results of the double-blind, placebo-controlled, independent clinical trials, and they offered a ninety-day unconditional guarantee. I was very impressed when I heard that they only offer their products through a network of conscious entrepreneurs who are rewarded for educating and empowering others to take responsibility for their own health and well-being.

They really are focused on rebuilding, repairing, and regeneration—not only for the human body, but also for sustainable businesses.

I felt immediate alignment with the culture of the company through the stories that were shared and I eventually had the pleasure of conversing with Bill Lee when I was a guest at Hilltop Gardens—the largest aloe plantation in the U.S. What a perfect setting to meet a man whose vision was big enough to hold my own.

I was strolling through the gardens, feeling a deep appreciation for the beautiful and colorful diversity of the hundreds of birds, flowers, and trees that surrounded me. It was a full-sensory experience to take it all in. My eyes welled with tears as I sat quietly in the Children's Garden and got up to quietly to enter the Healing Garden.

Of course, that's when I saw Bill heading my way.

"Renee! Welcome! Do you mind if I join you on your walk?" He fell into an easy stride beside me.

I was so inspired to have this one-on-one time, to get to know this man I had only seen at the corporate headquarters in Seattle, or at larger events in a major city.

"Bill, I love how you inherited your desire to bring the best of nature to humankind from your father. How did you know this would be your vision, too?"

He smiled at me as we stopped by the reflection pool to converse.

"Renee, I didn't know it until after I was studying for my PhD in Sociology, when I realized that we spent most of our time discussing the core factors that started various wars and looking back on history to solve today's conflicts. I saw that ultimately, I would end up being a professor talking about the past. It dawned on me that my father was truly bringing forth a wisdom he discovered through his relationship with nature, and that it was the healing properties of aloe that had extended his life by two decades. It became clear to me that if more people in our global society had this awareness, it would make a much bigger impact for social change than I could create as a sociology professor."

I nodded in agreement. "Once a teacher, always a teacher, even if you are not in a classroom. And this message of the healing properties of plants is an essential one for people to grasp today. I so appreciate that you are providing opportunities for people to learn this science and then pay it forward by sharing it with others in a conscious business model."

It was then that Bill shared that not only did he believe in bringing the best of nature to humankind, but that sharing the wealth with "the many" rather than "the few" was part of his long-term vision.

Inspired by his generosity, I responded, "Yes, I can see how we could also bring the best of humankind to nature at a time when too many businesses are not honoring any relationship with Mother Earth."

Being in his presence, I felt his heart of gold. Yes, he is a billionaire from South Korea. Yes, he inherited his wealth from his father who built his empire by rebuilding South Korea after the war. But if you ask Bill what he does for a living, he would tell you he is a farmer. And it was so refreshing to meet such a humble man, who had created sustainable farming in five climate zones, a plant-based pharmaceutical research company, a quality guaranteed manufacturing, and a distribution system and network that enables everyone to thrive.

After several interactions with key leaders, I knew that I could trust the plant research and the formulas to take my own health to the next level. And even more exciting, I also could leverage all of my past experience and integrate my coaching and leadership development to help others who want to bring forward a conscious entrepreneurial business model grounded in education and empowerment. For the vision I was holding about people accessing their full potential, they would need to deepen their awareness about the miraculous capacity of their body to heal.

I know that Univera showed up in my life because I had been on a mission to find a business that was about serving others and that valued education as a key component of its success.

I shared my vision with many who were driven to be of service to others, and they could see that this is a business that makes a difference. Realizing that the purpose of business is to solve problems, it was obvious that too many people do not know how to take back their personal power to feel better, look better, and perform better, and even alter the way we experience the aging process. By using the tools and processes, my team and I were grateful to co-create a team-based, turn-key business where one can be rewarded financially with residual income that can get them off the hours for dollars ride, provide them a willable asset as part of their legacy for future generations, and actualize natural vitality through regenerative nutrition.

For fourteen years, I have grown younger (just ask my doctors!) as I have helped build leadership teams, masterminds, and an ever-evolving learning community with well-being at the center. I know beyond a shadow of a doubt that as we experience our body as a living system—one in which all of our parts are interdependent—the more we become aware of how to nourish ourselves from the inside out with regenerative nutrition. This facilitates one's mental clarity to observe how we are also part of nature—an ecology of all living systems. It also becomes easy to experience the truth that when we integrate sustainable choices first with ourselves, then with our family and other key relationships, it becomes easier to bring it to our businesses, organizations, and government. To me, establishing a sense of individual well-being is central to learning who we are and why we are here, and to contributing to the overall collective well-being.

Out of all of my business experiences, Univera has been the most sustainable and duplicable. Through it,

I have cultivated relationships and resources that are allowing me to live my potential and help others do the same.

Looking through the rearview mirror, I can connect the dots. My experience of broken systems both in education, healthcare, and business drove me to keep asking the questions and looking for a better way—a true living system that is integrated and offers a way for each of us to bring our own unique genius to our life, find our gifts, and then give them to others in a sustainable way—physically, mentally, emotionally, and spiritually.

I had found a model of regenerating resources and systems and creating the sustainability that I hadn't been able to find in other places.

There was only one last piece that I had to put in place.

CHAPTER FIVE

Reaching Upward and Beyond with the Soul of Technology

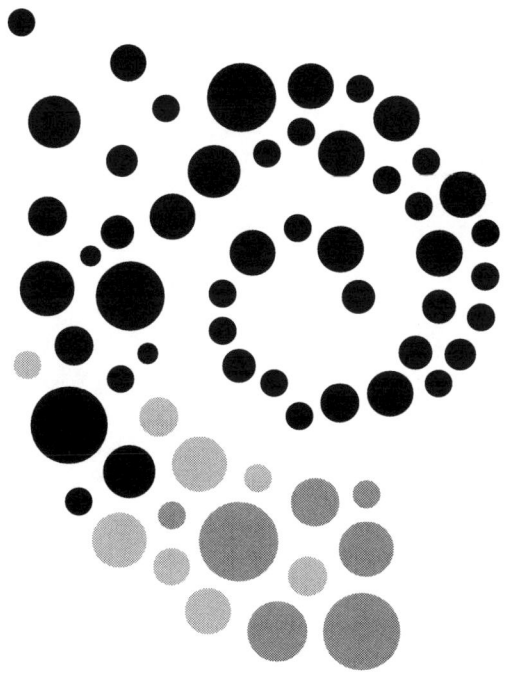

BRENT AND I spent several hours debriefing all that we'd learned from working with the Wondertree kids and their work with technology.

"They just took to it like a duck to water." He grinned from ear to ear. I, too, felt warm all over from the natural enthusiasm that bubbled out of these kids and into my heart.

"Yep, it is so awe-inspiring to be with kids who are so excited to innovate, create, and design. They use their genius without ever having to ask for permission." I looked around at the beautiful space that Wondertree had grown into and marveled at how different this environment was from everything else I had witnessed.

"Technology is definitely speeding everything up, Renee, and I continue to be amazed at how these self-directed learners are organizing what they want to learn, acquiring knowledge, and creating meaning for themselves every step along the way." Brent stood next to me, breathing in the magnitude of what was unfolding in this building and in the minds of the children there.

In my heart, I knew and said out loud: "And, if we don't adapt to this evolutionary process, we will definitely be left behind." I looked down at my hands as I thought about these kids. "You know, I see these kids as my teachers. They are the early adopters with the latest new software, and I have been learning from them how to actually use these tools most effectively."

"Yes. Me, too," Brent started. "Even though I am an innovator, partnering with these kids and observing how they organize their learning with the use of technology tools completely alters my thinking about how learning happens. I have been looking for ways to get off the linear conveyor belt, and these kids are affirming that with the proper use of tech tools, we can acquire knowledge in a meaningful way in an organic and natural process that transcends time. The integration of software tools with the latest hardware expands the whole learning experience and supports the creative expression of personalized learning. Kids can go as fast or as slow as they need to in order to understand what they are learning. The application is built right into attaining the knowledge."

Brent walked over to the large round table that the kids sat around every day to map out their plans and collaborate on their projects. I had noticed the mandala design painted on the table, but I had never understood how they were using it.

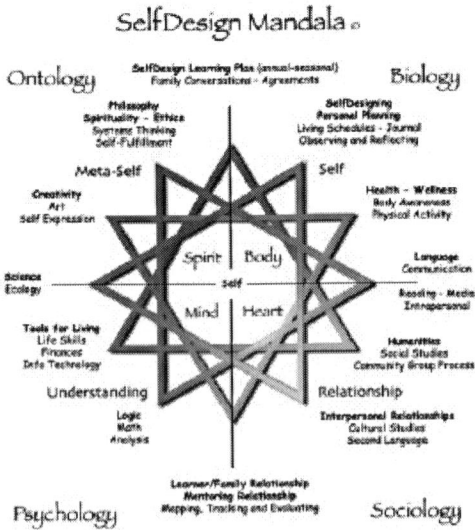

"You've seen the kids use this, right?" he asked as his hand grazed the table.

"Yes, but I haven't a clue how they use it. Do tell."

"The SelfDesign Mandala is a comprehensive map of learning opportunities. When we use this, we are not using it as a map of expectations, but a map of opportunities." Brent's enthusiasm for this tool and the learning it facilitated oozed from every pore as he continued. "This is a way for learners to map their understanding and apply it to the core subjects. It helps them understand multiple points of view simultaneously, and it is the foundational tool for vibrant discussions. You see, if we are to truly make meaning from the knowledge we acquire, we have to be in the center, the four quadrants of Spirit (top left), Body, (top right), and then Mind (bottom left), and Heart (bottom right)." He motioned to each quadrant as he named them.

I walked around the table and could see how the intersecting lines related to each other and all of them had that core of spirit, body, mind, and heart at the center. The key placeholders that emanated out from this core included self, relationship, understanding, and holism; and then the next level revealed ontology, biology, sociology, and psychology. I shook my head at the magnitude of the tool I was observing.

If I would have had a personal map that helped me organize my learning as I went through my 14,000 hours of schooling, I could have grown my awareness of who I am from the inside-out and seen more possibilities of how

I could interact in the world beyond schooling. It is pretty clear that the one-dimensional view of schooling, focused on the mind, is confused about where real learning occurs. Real learning unfolds in the personal reflection about the knowledge, which only becomes memorable to the person personally—through the heart and body— as they feel emotions and access the awareness that connects everything.

"This SelfDesign Mandela offers choice for each learner because each of us is a unique being in the universe. As different as snowflakes or fingerprints, we are each motivated to pursue journeys of unique desires and understandings. It seems absurd to require that everyone learn the same facts and skills. And it is with this map that each learner designs his/her learning plan, which organizes conversations and committees. So, you can see how they designed the PowerSmart software with this, right?"

"Yes! I can see exactly how they used it to organize their process and their teams. And now I know why they are so excited about their projects. It's all about empowerment, choices, and organizing towards a shared outcome where each chooses any area of learning being called forth."

Brent reinforced my understanding, "Yes, and each are free to choose or not choose any areas for learning. Parents are an integral part of the process and are invited to act as advisors and observers. Plus, we introduce mentors and resources to each learner and help them track their learning experiences throughout the year."

Seeing me deeply engrossed in the conversation, the learners took my hand and led me to their computer where they showed me another creation—a software program called the Map of Distinctions.

I understood the power of the integrative principle, but what they showed me next blew my mind—kids organizing knowledge with technology in a way that demonstrated the interconnectedness of life as we know it.

Brent stood beside me and explained as we watched the kids demonstrate. "It all started with a philosophical conversation about how the universe works and is organized. We wanted a map to show how it was all connected, so we could understand it, and I suggested that they each come up with fifty questions they were interested in exploring."

"Brent, I love how you always treat the kids as if they already know, and trust them to unfold their intelligence from the inside-out."

"Yes, and as a mentor, I knew there had to be a way to connect all of 'this curiosity' into essential categories, so I looked around for models of how other people had organized large bodies of knowledge."

"Guess that would be a good place to start. What did you discover?" I probed as I leaned forward to take in what was on the screen in front of me.

"Believe it or not, Renee, it was through locating the macropedia for the *Encyclopedia Britannica* that I noticed that all of the material there was organized into ten categories and formed a circle, stemming from the word encyclopedia, which suggested the meaning of circle or cycle. I reorganized them and added two more; everything (one) at the top and nothing (zero) at the bottom, which made twelve categories all together. The kids liked the idea."

I could see that the categories included: Matter and Energy, The Earth, Life on Earth, Human Life, Human Society, History, Fields of Knowledge, Technology, The Arts, Religion.

I looked sideways at Brent: "What did you do with the questions?"

"Well, that was interesting. We sorted the 500 questions into the same categories that we used the Mandala to organize. Then we created a large wall map of the twelve categories and related topics that branched off from the twelve areas. And for this age group (9-13), the areas of most interest were Life on Earth and human life. Most of their questions were about animals and nature."

"Yes, and then how did you integrate this into a software program?" I wondered aloud.

"This was learning at its best, as one goal moved us to the next. We bought a scanner and a microphone and added sounds to the computer program; and we wrote biographies of the famous people who interested us."

"It is amazing how the computer and the software you integrated became a vehicle to facilitate the project into a form—an actual product that the kids created, which they could bring to the marketplace."

"What is even more amazing is how many adults could not fathom how I played such a minor role, and how the kids could create such a complex and in-depth project on their own."

"How did it feel when you won the recognition for 'innovative use of technology in education?" I smiled again, remembering the kids' pride in this achievement.

"We were proud and it was the first of many. In fact, we actually received $5,000 as part of an award given to us for being one of the top four in elementary education; but truth be told, we knew the real fun and learning had come in creating the software and learning how to be programmers."

"What did you do with the money?" I asked.

"As a group, we decided to invest our winnings in the purchase of our first color computer to create video animation. We also, through consensus, made a decision to pay the kids between $40 and $80 each for their biographical works."

"Wow, that's fantastic. So, can you show me how this works?" I asked, trying to make sense of what I was looking at on the screen.

"Sure! Take the documentary of a time in history as an example. Remember when you and I were in school we learned history from a chronological perspective and also based on regions of the world, as in American History, Canadian History, etc.? Sometimes there would be special units on the WWI or WWII. You know—

memorize the facts and dates, pass the test, next." He paused and looked up with a humble smile. "Now, with this integrative approach, the learners could map out the symptoms leading to the war from the polar opposite viewpoints, the people impacted, the power struggle, the sacrifices, the financial impact of the battles, movement and displacement, the lessons learned, and legacy for a nation. Each of these topics, when integrated into a software program, has multiple links that deepens the associations. Learning history this way dynamically opens up a keen awareness that otherwise would be missed."

"Maybe by interacting with history, we can stop repeating history and finally get it right!" I exclaimed, unable to contain my excitement.

Brent was beaming. It was contagious. The kids were taking on all of their subjects with a vigor to show how, with technology, no textbook could ever replace their ingenuity.

"Find the Soul in Technology"

When the Oregon Charter School Bill did not pass, I was quite down-hearted that my dream of creating a Wondertree-inspired learning community could not be launched. I spent some time in deep reflection on what was next. And then, it came in a dream: "Find the soul in technology."

I woke up wondering, *Is that an oxymoron, or what? Does technology have a soul? What does it mean?*

I held the question close, waiting for answers to arise.

As I walked around Washington Park later that day and experienced the awakening of trees and flowers blooming in spring, I suddenly had an epiphany!

What if I look for technology companies in Portland that are engaged in the education arena and line up some informational interviews to research what they are doing, who they are serving, and how it might relate to my own quest for designing empowered learning communities?

I quickly found the perfect company, Pierian Spring Software, which was named after the spring found in Greek mythology where the muses would go and drink for inspiration. I arranged an informational interview where I more or less interviewed them to see if it would be a good fit for me to accomplish my mission to prove how technology could free up our industrial schooling framework. They felt my passion and welcomed me to their team of innovators.

I was hired on as Geography Product Manager and had the great pleasure of working with a team of designers who would create experiential learning programs that would inspire students to learn about their countries, states, cities, and towns, as well as mapping skills, diversity of cultures, geo-ecological components of the Earth, and more.

The overwhelming response of the students was very favorable and the technological element invoked a curiosity and discovery mindset that catalyzed the pursuit of learning in a way that the textbooks alone did not.

I'll never forget the first conference held by the National Geographers Association and American Association of Geographers. As I listened to the keynote speakers, I heard what I had been longing to hear from others about holistic learning: "Learning from a sense of place can expand to include all the other subjects in a way that integrates meaning through connection."

Up until this exposure, I had not experienced the psychology of geography, the science of geography, the mathematics of geography, the art of geography, the business of geography, and the sociology of geography.

"It's an organic approach to organizing knowledge within a flexible framework that makes the whole more than the sum of its parts."

Hearing this further supported what I had learned while working with Brent: Children learn more quickly and effectively when they follow their curiosity and work to solve problems that require an interdisciplinary approach. The problem is the current school system has a curriculum that has effectively separated the domains of knowledge. Math, English, and History all reside in their own domains, and it's rare that children experience how they intersect with each other in real-world problems.

Wow, it's as if the experts are arguing amongst themselves in isolation, and our children are stuck with what they think is important to know, reduced down to facts that will be memorized for the tests. They are required to regurgitate answers to someone else's questions that mostly ignore what the kids might be naturally curious about. Until this moment, I never realized that geography is a subject that naturally requires the intersection of these subjects.

When people have a sense of place, and experience their geography, as they explore the world around them—from neighborhoods to cities to states to countries—they discover diversity and similarity, a relationship to themselves and to each other, and then a deeper appreciation for nature herself. And of course, there are a myriad of opportunities to understand different cultures and experience their world, and solve problems that will naturally require them to solve math equations, acquire historical data, and record and communicate their findings in written language.

After the conference, when I returned to my role as Program Manager for Geography Software programs, I was so inspired to share what I had learned.

I could feel the deeper intention for our project emerge. As we put our heads and hearts together to create the storyboards that would become Continent Explorer and Interactive Geography, we were inspired to hold the bigger picture—how the soul of technology is to catalyze real-world learning that is meaningful, engaging, and fun!

One of my coworkers summarized it perfectly: "The students will naturally be integrating natural principles, cultivating their own core values as they virtually experience Planet Earth, following their natural curiosity, and experiencing the power of being guided by their own desire to want to know."

I nodded in agreement. "No matter where they go, it is this awareness that they will take with them as they explore beyond the current place that they call home."

Her eyes danced with the possibility. "When you think about it, these experiential programs put the kids in the driver's seat, and this is empowering them to own their learning, rather than being bored in someone else's vehicle with their hands tied and mouths gagged."

This company had an incredible idea, but the big challenge was that their primary customer—the school system—couldn't quite accept the idea of having the student in the driver's seat of their own adventurous explorations. The purchasing agents were looking for how this cutting-edge technology would work with the textbooks in each subject area; but since the textbooks were (on the average) seven years behind, it was a mismatch.

We were facing an unwilling audience who was not capable of making decisions that would rock the current paradigm, and we could not create inroads for what the students were seeking. The experts were, again, disconnected from the needs of their primary customers (the students) who were bored with the day-to-day, outmoded routines of outdated textbooks, worksheets, etc. There were technology solutions available to unleash the innovative minds, but the controlling paradigm would not adapt.

Needless to say, with the primary customer being education—with its lack of funding and receptivity to adopt innovative solutions—and the average cost of developing the discovery-based software being over $250K, the company had to close down.

Nevertheless, these experiences reinforced for me that technology was more than what it appeared to be. Unarguably, it provides tools that are catalytic for freeing up the natural enthusiasm for learning and also for life. Yet, by trying to fit twenty-first century technology into nineteenth century educational systems, we are missing what is dying to happen—a total transformation.

Sitting in my home office, feeling frustrated and discouraged, I rehashed everything I had learned about my own transformation over the last twenty years.

It is our relationships that matter, and when technology supports our true engagements, we will become more aware of our capacities to evolve. It will require meeting the true needs of our children and the future that they will be inheriting, which is a completely different world than the one we see today. Students need to discover themselves because if they can't be themselves, how will they ever unfold their full potential? Once they know themselves, they will inevitably start to ask questions like: Who am I? Why am I here? What are my questions, that I am curious to know the answers to?

Allowing the technology to be there as support for the students to collect knowledge and data to support their own inquiries would facilitate their natural enthusiasm. Teachers would become more of a guide than a disseminator of data because the technology can do that. The culture of classrooms would be kids excited about their quest and experiencing positive acknowledgment along the way.

I sat up straight at my desk, suddenly determined to continue working toward this dream.

Failure is not to be feared. Instead, it can be motivating to improve possibilities. What's a new and even more powerful way to achieve this?

That day, I created Living The Potential Network, to focus on integrating technology solutions, developing learning communities, and building a sustainable bridge between business and education.

Based on our societal contract, most businesses operate with the assumption that their up-and-coming employees—the products coming off the conveyor belt—aren't hirable until they graduate; but more and more are recognizing that no matter what degree the new graduates have acquired, they aren't ready for today's workplace. Yet the biggest tragedy of this whole story is that our kids are not only capable of so much more than what they are currently being asked to do, they are more able than most adults to solve problems when they know their strengths and are placed in environments that nurture them!

And this is true, especially when it comes to technology. Have you seen how quickly children figure out technology? I bet you have. In fact, if you're like most parents, you often find yourself handing your device to your child to figure out how to make it work.

Keeping Up with the Soul of Technology

IN THOMAS L. Friedman's latest book, *Thank You for Being Late: An Optimist's Guide to Thriving in the Age of Accelerations*, he brings to light the importance of technology and the speed of change as he shares the story of his exchange with Eric "Astro Teller," the CEO of Google's X Research and development lab, which produced Google's first self-driving car among other innovations. Teller is known as Captain of Moonshots, "turning what others would consider science fiction into products and services that could transform how we live and work."

According to Teller, "The speed of computing, the number of mobile devices, broadband connectivity and the latest cloud computing is accelerating and impacting almost every area of our lives."

With a deep understanding of the history of technology, Teller used the following graph to explain that, "by year 900 the process of technological and scientific change started to "speed up;" and the curve started to accelerate upward, highlighting how each generation of technology stands on its own shoulders. By 1900, it was taking twenty to thirty years for technology to take one step big enough that the world became uncomfortably different with something like the launch of the car and the airplane." Friedman continues to share Teller's reflection: "In 2016 that time window has continued to shrink. It's on the order of five to seven years from the time something is introduced to being ubiquitous and the world being uncomfortably changed."

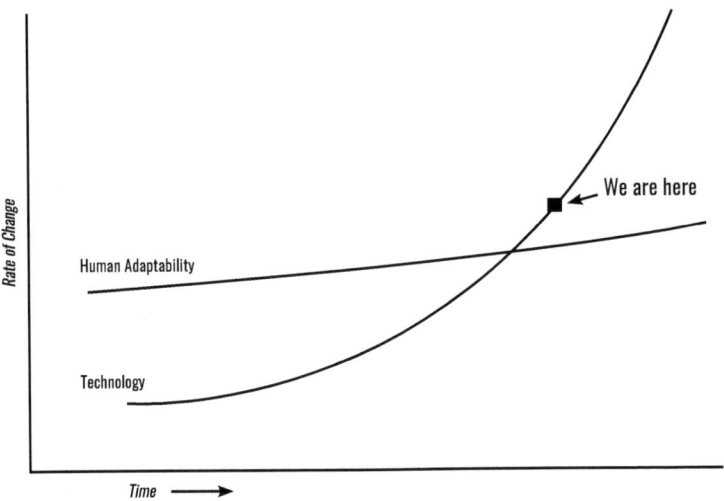

This is significant because even though human beings and many societies have steadily adapted to change, on average, the rate of technological change is now accelerating so fast that it has risen above the average rate at which most people can absorb all these changes.

How do we prepare ourselves, let alone our children, for this world? We can't stop it; we have to respond to it. It's like trying to ride a bike—you can't do it standing still, you have to get on it and move. Unless we begin working together to shift our paradigm and create new pathways to help us adapt and evolve our capacity to manage change—and live the potential of what it means to evolve—we might not be able to keep up.

Which is why we need to let the children lead us.

The Indian physicist, Sugata Mitra, from New Delhi, created an experiment in 1999, where he cut a hole in the brick wall that separated his office space from the slum that was right next door. In this hole, he installed a computer, with the screen and track pad facing the slum. As he describes, he connected the computer to the internet, added a browser, and walked back to his office. "These kids did not speak English, were unfamiliar with computers, and certainly had no knowledge of the internet; yet within days, not only did they figure out how to move the mouse, they accessed the internet and were teaching each other how to surf the web." Since then, this experiment has been replicated not only throughout India but all over the world, always with the same outcome: kids in small groups who were self-directed and unsupervised and without any formal training could learn to use computers very quickly and with a great deal of proficiency. Mitra eventually took a job as a professor of education at the University of Newcastle in England where he has developed a new primary school education which he calls "minimally invasive education." One of the outcomes from this pursuit is the SOLES project—Self-Organized Learning Environments— which now exists in several countries throughout the world.

Could this be a precursor to how we need to shift our view about education practices? Maybe it need not be top down from an expert or sage on the stage, but instead student-driven. Rather than kids learning on their own and competing with their classmates, it could be collaborative. It could be fun, and challenging, and constructive.

In fact, what if we leveraged what we've learned while watching kids play with video games? Since children are totally engrossed in their virtual game-playing adventures, if we gamified the educational learning environment and tapped into the students' focus, problem-solving skills, and ability to collaborate with others, we'd likely have more academic success with more students.

So maybe instead of teachers using classroom time to deliver lectures, students could bring their questions to class based on the YouTube videos (think Khan Academy) they watched the night before. Spirited discussions and projects would emerge, and kids would be inspired to solve problems and earn points along the way. The more they participate, the more points they would earn; and as in the game environment, the person with the most badges becomes known as a viable contender. Learning is fun and addictive when there is a challenge and we can bring ourselves to it.

At our current speed of change, we *all* must learn adaptive solutions. Some will say we are on the cusp of the Conceptual Age (or the Age of Imagination) and if so, it definitely requires an upgrade to our "already thinking."

According to Daniel Pink, in his book, *A Whole New Mind: Moving from the Information Age to the Conceptual Age*, "We are moving from an economy and a society built on the logical, linear, computer-like capabilities of the Information Age to an economy and a society built on the inventive, empathetic, big picture capabilities of what's rising in its place—the Conceptual Age."

Those who are looking for how they will create a livelihood based on what they learned in school, may need to look long and hard about what is now being outsourced to other countries for a lower wage, and also what can now be taken over by technology. With driverless cars, self-propelled vacuum cleaners, and voice-activated remote controls, it seems it will absolutely be the right brain aptitude that will keep us humans in control of a mechanized society.

From *Sustainable Education: Re-Visioning Learning and Change*, by Stephen R. Sterling, we can see that Art leads Science by ten years, Science leads Business by ten years, and Business leads Education by ten years. So, what if we were able to integrate a holistic approach that blended these typically separate domains and engaged both hemispheres of the brain at the same time? In an integral way of being, this would be assimilated naturally, especially as we were called to express beyond our segmented domains of expression.

Daniel Goleman's work in *Emotional Intelligence (EQ)* has examined an array of academic studies that have attempted to assess IQ, which measures the Left-Directed thinking prowess and how it accounts for career success—and guess what he discovered? What we have been measuring only accounts for between 4%–10% of career success. It may help you get the job, but keeping the job will require more of the right brain because, according to Goleman, "Neither side of the brain can do the job without the other—the left is about 'text' and the right is about 'context.' We know that the left directed, IQ-focused way of learning is no longer sufficient. We must bring forth the aptitudes emanating from the right brain hemisphere—the artistry, empathy, taking the long view, pursuing the transcendent."

Yes, technology is *a huge* part of our lives today, and it's up to us to bring forth the essence of what makes us human and what can never be outsourced to a robot. Let's face it—if you want to learn about a topic, you Google it to see what's out there, or you may use *Wikipedia* to understand further and perhaps contribute to the knowledge base, or you may be using Skype where you can see and talk with people around the world, or perhaps you have chosen to use Zoom as an interactive platform for bringing many people together where you can see and speak with each other and move into different rooms to collaborate in smaller groups and then come back to the larger group to share what you've discovered.

The answer is *not* technology—*it is our relationship with technology and its ability to enhance our human relationships that is being called forth. It is the* **soul** *of technology.* Somehow, we are missing this, and it is quite noticeable when we observe people so absorbed by their smart phones that they become oblivious to the person sitting across from them at the dinner or the conference table.

The key capabilities for the twenty-first century are critical-thinking, collaboration, creativity, and problem-solving. They have become the new version of the three R's (reading, writing, and arithmetic).

Technology can bring us the information—the facts are there—and what do we do with it is the new focus. It is up to us to develop the key questions that need to be answered during this great time of change.

A Real Life Example

In my current work with Living The Potential Network, I am determined to create a living, breathing example of what is possible when we cross-pollinate sectors that are currently divided internally and collectively.

My mission is to connect entrepreneurial parents, growth-minded teachers, and forward-thinking businesses to engage the wisdom of our youth and work together to save the world.

With the use of the Core Value Index, I am helping people develop an awareness of their inner wiring and technology. I create and facilitate fertile, self-directed learning environments, using live and virtual settings with the help of the Zoom platform, which allows me to connect with people all over the world to help them increase their health and well-being with Univera products and masterminds and coaching. I am able to connect people via Zoom and conference calls to meet each other, learn from each other, and discover their capacity to leverage their gifts and talents to help others who are looking for those resources. Through these relationships came the idea of twenty-first century mentoring and how to implement this platform to bridge the gap between business and education. This pursuit keeps all of us working at our leading edge.

As a co-host for the radio show Pathways (streamed via KBOO FM), a show about personal and cultural transformation, I invite key leaders to share their wisdom in ways where we can grow our awareness and know that people are gaining valuable insights and tools to feel better and do better for themselves, their families, and the world.

Five years ago, before he made his final transition, Brent asked if I would become the Chair of SelfDesign Foundation and support the vision we shared into its highest possibility. And much of that is coming true with the SelfDesign Graduate Institute which is a holistic, post-modern, integral, low residency-high relational Master's in Holistic Education. Here we have learners from around the world and with the Zoom platform, we are able to connect as if we are all in the same room. These learners are leaders who are committed to the holistic education movement and who will become the facilitators not only in public schools and in designing private learning communities, but also in learning organizations within businesses and non-profit organizations. Because we engage in the lifelong learning paradigm, we offer pathways for public schools to learn and develop personalized learning processes as well as engage our elders who are not retiring but who are self-designing their elderhood.

Through our smart use of technology, we are accessing each other's wisdom from the sacred space that this technology supports.

The Power of Place – An Invitation

As I look back at my journey through education, the medical industry, business, and technology, it's easy for me to see that I have been operating from the *paradigm of place*. No matter the sector or industry, I followed my curiosity and solved the problems before me; and despite a difficult start in life, I have found my place. I am choosing to trust the seeds of change, cultivate fertile learning environments, cross-pollinate domains, create sustainability with regenerative resources and systems, and reach upward and beyond with the soul of technology.

By now, you can see my dream of helping children and adults identify their seeds of genius and then nurture them with supportive learning environments. You have seen the power of the cross-pollination of education and business with the story of Wondertree and LearningWare Software, Inc. You know that in order to create long-term change, we have to make sure that we are creating sustainability in ourselves and in our systems. And, you have seen the power of technology to help us do this.

All that's left are these questions:

- Who are you? What are your strengths and values? What do you care about? Are you aware of your innate nature, where it is easy to design your life from the inside out, based on your wiring and core capacities?

- Where do you have influence? Are you an entrepreneurial parent, whose child is weary of an archaic industrial age education system? Are you wanting to find or create something more nurturing and supportive for them? Are you a teacher who is tired of the info-in-info-out approach to education—who wishes that you could create a more nurturing, self-directed environment for your students? Are you a business person who is afraid of what's going to happen if the education system doesn't find a way to prepare kids for the challenges they are going to face when they get hired by a company like yours? Are you a lover of well-being and sustainability, and nature, and technology— and hungry to find a way to do something meaningful for the next generation?

- What if there were a heart-centered mentoring approach organized through a master mind network of people who are choosing to learn for life? And what if these mentors were skilled in listening and facilitating positive change for themselves and others in ways that supported the upgrades needed for our future leaders to thrive?

These key inquiries have unleashed some strategic pathways that can only strengthen our resolve to integrate innovative solutions for moving from where we are to our highest and best possible outcomes.

We need parents, teachers, business owners, and leaders to emerge from every sector and say "yes" to a vision of everyone living the potential in order to create a world that our children will thrive in.

Will you say "yes"?

Engaging the Wisdom of Our Youth Saves Their Lives and the World

NOW THAT YOU have experienced the five steps of engaging the wisdom of our youth to save the world, I want to share something special with you.

While writing this book, I reached out to several of the Wondertree learners from the days when I was working with Brent and the PowerSmart entrepreneurs; and I asked them if they would be willing to share how their time at Wondertree has impacted their lives.

Just as I am sure you are, I was curious about the long-term impact an experience like this would have on their personal and professional well-being, as well as the industries in which they chose to invest themselves.

Here are the questions I asked them during our conversations and summaries of each one.

Note: Wondertree later became Virtual High (VH), so these names are used interchangeably throughout the summaries.

Questions for Wondertree/Virtual High Learners:

- What was the biggest gift in your experience of the Wondertree/Virtual High learning?

- How has that environment contributed to your life and career success?

- In what specific ways and/or situations have you seen that this learning environment gave you an edge that those coming out of the "traditional" educational system don't have?

- How have you replicated the elements or principles of that learning environment in your work/business/career? Can you give an example?

- If you have children, how does your experience at Wondertree/Virtual High contribute to your parenting and education approach with them?

Ilana Cameron was actually the catalyst for the birth of Wondertree. As the only daughter of Brent and Maureen Cameron, she was given the opportunity to design her own learning from a very early age. When it came time to choose which school she would attend, Ilana and her parents visited several schools and interviewed teachers along the way. There is a picture of her sitting on a swing after one of the interviews and, as Brent told the story, "It was while swinging on that swing that Ilana very clearly articulated that 'if she went into that building, she would lose herself forever.'" That's when Brent, Maureen, and Ilana planted the seeds that eventually grew into Wondertree and then matured into Virtual High.

For Ilana, the biggest gift of the Wondertree and Virtual High experience was being respected as a full participant in her learning environment, and feeling a sense of ownership of that space because of her level of involvement in the day-to-day running of Wondertree. This gave her a different frame to her learning. "We were a community, not a school; and this created a space for us to thrive and fully engage in all aspects of our educational experience," she said.

Ilana understands that learning happens because it is in our nature as humans to be curious about ourselves and the world. When we make respectful relationships the important part of the process, all the other educational components fall into place easily. The students learned multiple subjects by completing projects, rather than segmenting into different subjects. This vibrant, integrated experience of many topics is one of the amazing contributions Virtual High made to her life and to so many others.

Because of this experience at Virtual High, Ilana approaches all of her growth with enthusiasm and attempts to make things better for those around her, engaging others in the delight she feels for the world. As for the edge this experience gave her over others who were schooled more traditionally, she explains that it is the ability to be resourceful and respond to situations, rather than just reacting without seeing the bigger picture.

Ilana currently works in specialty coffee as a roaster and started her own company in 2016. When she attends work conferences, she finds it natural to connect with people and create community. She has found that all of the skills she has gathered over the years make sense and can be dynamically integrated. In 2015, when she went to the International Women's Coffee Association (IWCA) brunch and happened to sit beside two of the most skilled and famous female roasters in the United States, she befriended and continues to build upon those relationships today.

As I listened to her, I realized what a powerful experience it must be to walk through the world and meet people with a deep sense of community and collaboration. Can you imagine sitting next to someone who is the best at the game, and feeling like there is no reason you couldn't be in relationship with or partner with them to do something greater?

I believe that is the true gold that came out of VH— the experience of collaborating with people younger, older, and much older—and developing this deep sense of knowing one's place in that environment and every one that comes after it.

Jesse M. Blum, PhD received many gifts from Virtual High, including truly unique amazing experiences, considerable opportunities to step up and grow, and lifelong relationships with wonderful people. Jesse dove into a wide variety of activities that VH had to offer, and co-created many of them himself. He engaged across the board, whether it was participating in big weekly group meetings where the community of learners ruled by consensus; engaging with city architects and developers to help research and develop Village Quest; waiting tables during the community-hosted coffee nights; co-authoring the Learning-a-Living report on VH to the Canadian federal government; grant writing to fundraise for multimedia equipment; working on all-night software development sessions; shooting video and editing it for various projects; contributing to the Wondernet; doing dishes; giving talks in public arenas in front of hundreds of attendees; teaching adults how to use the World Wide Web; playing Halushka (in-house developed sport most favored by VHers for its inclusivity); giving radio and television interviews; taking college-level philosophy and psychology courses; presenting awards to Jane Goodall, Noam Chomsky, and Michael Moore; shadowing legal and business mentors, sitting on the Wondertree board of directors; co-developing the InsightOut WonderTree program for 18–24 year-olds; or just having great conversations for hours on end with his friends. Jesse fostered relationships with his fellow learners and mentors, many of whom he remains in contact with to this day. For Jesse though, Virtual High transcended a schooling experience and became a way of life—one that he continues to practice to this day. To him, VH is a never-ending journey that is summed up by the greatest gift it offered him— the courage to say "yes." For Jesse, Virtual High is the ongoing courage needed to say "yes" and follow the path that is the most right in the moment.

VH provided Jesse with key opportunities to take responsibility for his life. He used these to build upon the solid foundations instilled in him by his loving parents, previous educational experience, and most importantly, his core essence. As a result, Jesse sees his life as an ongoing process of discovery of that essence through various roles that he takes on—from being a professional software engineer, project manager, and grant writer, to his travels and the experiences of becoming a husband and a father.

Today, Jesse lives in Belgium with his wife and the youngest of his three children. His eldest is eighteen and, like him, moved out early. His middle daughter lives in Scotland with his ex-wife during the school year and lives with him during the holidays. When I asked him about his approach to parenting, he said that he respects his children and their journeys. He always meets them at their eye level, even if that means getting on the ground. And he has always asked himself how he can learn from them and vice versa. While he is not trying to be their friend, he is entirely motivated by his love for them and sees himself as one of their most important mentor/learning consultants, which again reflects the Virtual High ethics. He proudly stated, "It's incredible to watch them grow from the inside out."

Jesse holds a PhD in Computing Science from the University of Stirling in Scotland as well as a BSc in Software Systems Engineering from there. Before moving to the UK, and a few years after VH, he received a diploma in video game programming. Following a post-doc at the Horizon Digital Economy Research Institute of the University of Nottingham, he now works as a Data Scientist for one of the largest insurance companies in the world. He also has been published in the *Philosophical Transactions of the Royal Society* (oh, by the way, Isaac Newton was published there too!), as well as in about twenty other peer-reviewed publications on topics ranging from digital home-based psychiatric monitoring, to e-infrastructure for social science, to artist mediated participatory sensing for environmental discourse, to citizen empowerment through collaborative sensemaking, to the ethics of using wearable cameras in public.

Living the Virtual High way has been distinctly non-linear for Jesse. Over the years, his adventures have taken him from the Pacific Northwest to presenting VH at the first Ecovillage conference in Findhorn, Scotland, to working as a migrant picker on a tomato farm in the middle of the Negev Desert, to working as a laborer in a tent and tarp factory; from intermediating between designers, developers and customers of content-managed websites, to academic excellence, to financial data analytics, and even a bit of entrepreneurship. He laughed as he reminisced, "It's been a strange journey. Maybe I should have been more conventional, but then I wouldn't have a PhD and be living in the heart of Europe!" He has clearly given himself permission to be the author of his own life.

Jesse loves asking questions and, as he calls it, digging. A lot of this skill was cultivated at Virtual High, and he acknowledges that this form of learning is part of his essence. In his view, people who accept conventional answers get mediocre results; but for himself, he wants to really know what's going on. "Replication of the VH learning and production environment is a bit hard," Jesse remarked. "We had a high level of expectations coming out of VH. They were our norm, but it's not the norm."

Jesse's approach in the business arena is to lead by example. He often offers his colleagues interesting strategies to solve problems. VH provided a couple more gifts that help in this process—consensus mentality and patience. Though it's tough to bring new ideas to a culture that doesn't naturally think outside of the box, he believes in the approach called the Nudge Theory, which is based on a Pulitzer Prize-winning idea. He said that it's how he engages—not like a bull in a china shop, but more stealthy like a ninja—that keeps challenging sacred cows (the status quo) and providing solutions that nudge his organizations forward. Through Jesse, Virtual High continues to spread courage into these organizations with the courage to say "yes," take leaps, pay attention, and keep learning.

Travis Bernhardt sometimes wonders, "What if I hadn't gone to Virtual High?" He really did not like public school and left after grade ten. He did not attend university, and said that if he had, he might have pursued philosophy or law. In his twenties, after leaving Virtual High, he didn't have engaging relationships like he'd had as part of the VH learning community. Without those, he became depressed, missing the connection to a community of like-minded people and also not knowing how to stay self-directed in a world that prescribes university, careers, and families as logical next steps for anyone that age. When he went searching for what interested him, he rediscovered the online magic community. He'd always loved magic and had a natural talent for performing arts, and this community opened up a new path for engagement. Today, Travis is a magician. He performs in corporate shows, street shows, and festivals. He appreciates that he doesn't have to do what some boss tells him to do, as he never has respected arbitrary authority. He remembers when he was a kid in school and teachers tried to keep him from climbing structures around the school. He was always fine, but he couldn't persuade his teachers that he would be okay and felt like their authority was motivated by power and not genuine concern for his safety. Those early power struggles have informed his relationship with authority ever since. He shared that the greatest gift of his time at VH was his immersion in a community of idealists who showed him that *another way is possible*. This experience has shaped his entire worldview, from politics to relationships to his work as a performer.

Devon Girard said it was compelling to put together tasks and functions to see the results as a ten-year-old at Wondertree; and working with the early MacIntosh computer took the experience to a whole other level. The group had a project. They had a mission. It was like they were on a hero's journey. They were also being taken seriously by adults and had a business that impacted their self-talk. Devon shared: "You know, how other people see you is how you see yourself; and Brent took us and what we were doing seriously."

Devon said his experience at both Wondertree and Virtual High created a baseline for him when it came to finding energy for the day. There was something meaningful about each project and effort, and that experience still influences how he makes choices about where to put his energy. Devon also reflected on how an element of playfulness was an important component in their work: "If it feels like playing, then it seems easy and energizing, and I always want more of that. Isn't that a key to joy?"

He shared how, in one sense, there was no plan that could properly prepare any of them for life because life is surprising and disappointing...and it is all about unfolding things.

For example, he became a technology employee for a while and developed a serious repetitive stress injury, finding himself unable to do other things he wanted to do. He discovered that sometimes breakthrough moments come with a little bit of pressure—like being on a vision quest with the need to survive. And, to use Devon's words: "I get the push to find myself." This ethic was developed in him during his time at Virtual High where he learned how to accept uncertainty, and discovered how perseverance can pay off in the long run.

Later as he became a man, taking on adult responsibilities, and navigating myriad logistical challenges, there have been times of deep questioning—of not knowing. But today, he is at about 95% living his dreams and 5% asking the question, "What if I had done it differently?"

Devon talked about the risk in needing too much control or structure—how he wanted to do things on his own, but not alone. To explain his ideas, Devon used the example of the middle road that Buddhism refers to—being highly engaged without resisting or attaching. Whether it be climbing a mountain or doing a project, his risk assessment is related to when he might fall out of balance.

In Devon's day-to-day life, he is on a small repair crew of the local internet service provider out in the rural area of British Columbia, that helicopters out into the mountains. They make a good team as they learn on-the-job to deal with the day's problems.

Maybe it's harder to tell if he has an edge because of his self-directed life, but he does notice a difference in his *process.* For example, when presented with a problem or opportunity, Devon is confident that he can learn something. He can look at a situation and even if he doesn't understand it, he knows he will need new knowledge. He is comfortable with this and will scan the situation for clues that he can use as reference points to facilitate "on-demand learning." Watching others, he sees their reaction often is one of discomfort. "In other words, if we all decided to build a submarine and no one knew how to do it, I might be one of those who is just more comfortable learning how to figure something out."

He spoke about how the VH learners explored topics relevant to society, and then experienced history while integrating other bodies of work. In alignment with the truth that the whole is more than the sum of its parts, the experience was more than what appeared as the project or task at hand. To Devon, it was all about learning skills, connecting with others, and finding themselves. As he said, "Somehow all of our learning had this foundational element."

There was a spiritual component to this as well, which isn't always easy to articulate. Yet Devon reflected that, "If we allow children some self-direction in a safe place, they're more likely to grow up thinking the world is a safe place and their values will develop in that context." In a place like this, they realize for themselves that they wouldn't be able to live with themselves if they somehow became a greedy capitalist. They wouldn't feel good about it if they participated in oppression dynamics. They won't necessarily buy into the "me versus you" or the "us versus them" paradigm. As for him, coming out of a supportive childhood, where he was encouraged to be self-directed, he explained that he did feel some pressure to be the best he could be, but that it was internal in nature and different than trying to do the right thing out of fear of force. And for that, he is grateful.

Katie McCabe and Joseph Muncaster met at Virtual High, married many years later, and now have two sons. They own a computer business called Full Solution Computers. With a team of three other employees, they "make computers make sense." The only full-service computer specialty store in the area, Full Solution Computers offers repair, tutoring, and built-to-order systems, designed with the human in mind.

Katie reflects that the biggest gift from her time at Virtual High was personal empowerment. She had the awareness that she was clever, but that learning environment helped her to become a problem-solver and gave her the courage to take control of her life. She had been homeschooled for twelve years before she went to Virtual High, and she knew it was time for her to get out of her home "laboratory" to further develop her confidence, emotional ability, and capacity to get along with others. She knew she could learn and she had never lost the joy of learning; and VH showed her how to foster that joy and how to find information she needed when she needed it.

She trusted her curiosity about taking on new possibilities, which eventually inspired her to go to culinary school.

Katie also said the VH environment helped her to express her creativity. Before attending, she used to draw paper dolls in pencil crayon and developed an artist practice. In addition to going to culinary school, she started making and selling jewelry. In her words: "I kept being interested and had the time to explore, and I practiced what I was interested in." Eventually, she took an interest in bookkeeping because she likes numbers, and she handles that for their business. In her spare time, she volunteers on several local boards and continues to pursue her interest in the arts.

Joseph came to VH interested in journalism and writing, and he began to focus on computers as a tool to reach those goals. He had never used a Mac computer before; but whenever he felt lost, he would get all his questions answered, accelerating his learning. He always had the help he needed, which opened up his mind to what he could do when back home. Everyone wanted him to help them with their computer problems, and he was able to share what he had learned with others.

"A lot of who I am came from this learning environment. As a homeschooled teen, I often felt different from others my age. Going to VH connected me to a group of people who understood me, laughed at my jokes, and held up my ideas. It was life-changing for sure."

Katie added that in the classes she has taken since VH, where there has been a blend of adult learners of all ages, it has been interesting to observe how most of these students have addressed homework. Many people felt they didn't have to do it. She surmised, "Maybe it's when people feel like they are out of control and being told what to do that they resist it;

and it seems like they don't learn out of their own resistance." What she notices about herself is that she looked forward to doing the homework because she enjoys learning.

She loves the idea of lifelong learning and doesn't get burned out. If she wants to learn something, she can do it. It's a whole new way of thinking about life.

Joseph added that there are a lot of industries that are rigid, but the tech culture celebrates and rewards self-learning and individualism. This culture elevates original thinking, which has helped him run his own business for over twenty years. He easily teaches others problem solving approaches without ever having been "officially" trained for it, largely because his experience at VH helped him with out-of-the-box thinking.

Students from traditional education tend to label themselves as stupid or dumb and judge themselves harshly like, "I am not good at math or music," reiterating words that an unconscious teacher may have said to them. Joseph has always felt that people are inherently smart and that anyone can learn. He has used his passion to break down barriers and teach hundreds of people how to use computers, including seniors in their eighties. He has pursued his interests, and now he is in the industry that he loves. What he has noticed throughout his career is that the people who were good at school, and who were conditioned by standardized testing, didn't get a chance to "*learn about learning.*"

Joseph explained how the VH environment was a structured way of having no structure, and the same day never happened twice. It was more idea-driven, as in project-driven.

Joseph and Katie enjoy their two boys, witnessing their unique learning and strengths unfold. They are adamant about paying attention to what their children want to learn. With their youngest, it's all about stories and creativity; their oldest focused more on letters and numbers. Both Katie and Joseph are clear that everyone learns differently. They feel that their responsibility as parents is to develop opportunities for learning, and they spend time with them individually.

When their eldest was two years old, he started noticing license plates and reading off the letters of all the plates he saw. So, that's how he learned his numbers and letters. Katie and Joseph used everyday opportunities for learning, instead of saying, "We are going to learn to read now."

They hang out with other parents who are interested in learning and bring their kids to events, and they rejoice at how comfortable their boys are interacting with people of all ages. In fact, they shared a story about how recently they took their boys (age four and six) to a waste management event, where they were interested and asking questions about the garbage trucks and commenting on what they heard; and the adults around them were amazed.

Virtual High not only helped them to become happy, successful human beings, it set the stage for them to connect, marry, and now raise more healthy, happy, and successful learners.

THE MOVEMENT HAS BEGUN

Exciting Approaches to Changing the World

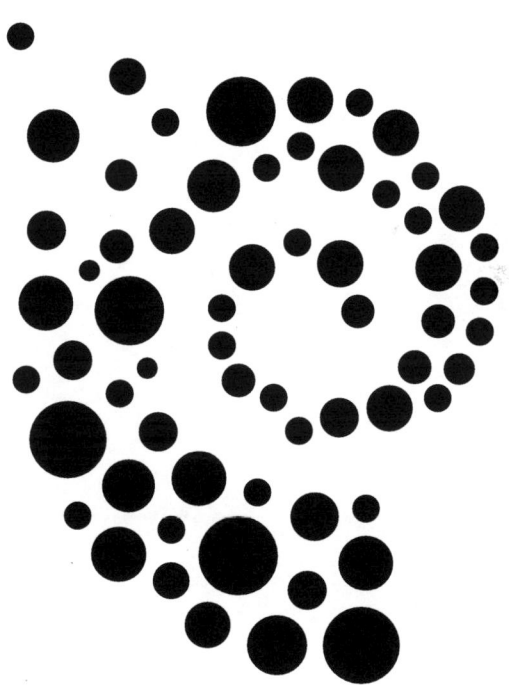

As I have been building the Living The Potential Network, I have crossed paths with some amazing souls who have been inspired to change a corner of the world with their particular seeds of genius. Our conversations and interactions have proven to me that I am not the only one dreaming about and working toward a better future for our children and our planet.

These folks are already developing new ways of tackling some of the problems I have discussed in this book with one or more of the elements of the *Living The Potential* framework; and I wanted to share a few of them with you to show you how incredible their work is and give you a sneak peek at how leveraging other parts of this model could enhance or accelerate their results.

This is the true mission of the Living The Potential Network—to connect people like *you* with people and organizations like these, so that we can all bring more of who we are to what we do and find ways to engage the wisdom of our youth along the way.

Trusting the Seeds of Change
Village Home Resource Center

VILLAGE HOME BEGAN in 2002 with founder Lori McKee Walker, who was motivated to design a community-learning environment for her two daughters. I will never forget our first meeting when I showed up on her doorstep and offered to be part of her founding board of directors. I knew what it took to create an "out-of-the-box" learning environment, and I wanted to be part of a team of people who were committed and courageous enough to make it happen. Trusting the seeds of change starts with the recognition that we are in the midst of a major societal shift and that deepening our understanding of how we nurture and support our progeny has everything to do with creating a positive future.

Village Home functions like a community college, starting at preschool. Families choose to take one class a week or take several a day to meet their education goals. They have diverse approaches to education and widely varied educational philosophies. Village Home believes that every learner is unique and deserves a unique education, as well as a community of people with whom to grow and learn.

The guiding principle that has underlined the success of Village Home is that the parent is included, and the family is honored, openly acknowledging that the parent is after all the first and primary educator for their children. With this belief, it was essential to have a family-friendly environment, a play space for younger siblings, and multi-age classrooms where siblings and parents and their children can learn together. Village Home values the parents as the primary influence for education and then sees itself as a resource center and secondary supportive environment.

Another guiding principle is that learning only happens in the context of self-direction. Intrinsically motivated, learners become authors of their own learning experience.

While Village Home offers classes in the areas of art, computers and technology, drama, history, language arts, math, music, PE, and dance, science, foreign language, social studies, and geography, it's the interdisciplinary and project-oriented classes and activities that are very popular. Some examples of interdisciplinary classes in the past have been literature seminars on books, such as *Harry Potter* or *Lord of the Rings* that bring science, art, drama, language arts, and history into the classroom around a common theme. "Math Artistry," which weaves geometry and other math disciplines into visual arts, is another popular course.

Village Home faculty relies on learners to measure their own success, and does not use grading tools. Learning is for the sake of learning.

Fast forward to the present.

There are three campuses and over 700 learners who are thriving in this learning community. What makes it work is their Choice-Based Learning Market-place. The learners get to choose what they want to learn and design their schedule. Parents are the managers of their children's education, and, in most cases, learners engage in learning activities outside of

Village Home. The faculty is experienced, passionate, and knowledgeable about their subject area. Many professionals, such as master gardeners, museum quality artists, or engineers, are eager to share their wisdom and talent to inspire others. One can create a course and apply to offer it, and once approved the families can enroll in an open registration. The average class size is 8-15 learners, which makes it possible to meet the self-directed needs of the individuals in the classroom. These are multi-age classrooms, where group and project-based learning is encouraged. Although the courses are non-credit and non-graded, the learners develop their own learning portfolios that support their entrance into college if that is the path they choose. As a matter of fact, many of the teens within Village complement their learning with courses at the local community college, earning credit for their high school diplomas and future degree.

It has been sixteen years since I met Lori Walker, and I have witnessed her vision grow and thrive. Many parents are realizing how their children unfold their natural intelligence in such a fertile environment where learning is challenging and fun. These learners love learning, and it is evident in so many ways, such as the competitions they have participated in on a local, state, and national level. Village Home learners have competed successfully at the regional, state, and national levels against traditionally educated peers in team competitions such as Mock Trial, Science Bowl, Lego Robotics, International Thespians, Destination

Imagination, and First Tech Challenge. A number of students perform regularly in professional theater and dance productions. Village Home has had Spelling Bee, Poetry Out Loud, GeoBee, and history bee competitors win and represent the school regionally and nationally. Most recently, one of Village Home's three Mock Trial teams won the Oregon State Championship and competed at Nationals. The VH Drama Department puts on at least two major productions at each of its campuses every year. The community of parents, faculty, learners, and even alumni align efforts to accomplish the sets, the costumes, and the promotional marketing.

I attended the most recent play *The Lion King, JR edition*. It was mind-blowing to see more than fifty kids, ages ten to fifteen, dancing and singing effortlessly with the style and grace of seasoned actors. Having been a drama director in a previous career, I have huge respect for Whitney Johnson and her capacity to teach these players how to trust the process—first for themselves in their roles, but also with each other in the various scenes. As she acknowledged the entire cast at the end of the play, they all had to trust the unknown as they worked over three months to put together every detail of the production as a team; and they didn't have access to the actual stage until a few days before with only eight hours of practice before opening night. Yet, because they were committed and each one knew their part, their trust in themselves and each other manifested in their best performance with a standing ovation from the audience that was tearful in appreciation of what they had just witnessed. "It takes a village" is more than a concept "to raise a child"; it's a state of being that I wish every parent would feel for themselves.

From my perspective, Village Home provides a pathway for parents to be more engaged in their children's learning for life. It's beyond schooling. Because of our fast-changing world and the impact of technology, designing learning environments where people can discover what we need to learn in order to adapt and evolve beyond our current normative culture is more essential than ever before. This learning environment provides a hybrid model that includes the family, the learners, and the faculty with a trans-disciplinary approach; the integrated knowledge students need for today's world; and collaborative processes to facilitate who they will need to become to save the world.

The youth are the catalyst and our inspiration, so why would we not include them? It's truly time we stop outsourcing the education of our youth without a renewed partnership with the most important stakeholders—the children, the parents, and other community members.

Recently, I attended a Village Home Celebration event where several students entertained the audience with improv and then shared what Village Home has meant to them. As I looked around the audience, I felt the respect and appreciation for the message that these young men and women were sharing. One young man was so impressive, I asked him for a copy of his speech so I could share it here with you.

My name is Anteo Ramirez, and I am a learner at Village Home. Thank you so much for having me here. I have come here to talk about learning and to speak about my experiences in both public school and at Village Home, which is a self-directed learning community.

Choice is a major part of education, at least from my experience, because when one chooses to learn, they are in control of what they want to become. My aspiration has always been to contribute in some way with the exploration of space; and when I take classes like Cutting Edge, and hear about spaceX launching the largest rocket since the Saturn V, I want to learn even more.

Village Home inspires students to follow and reach for their dreams. When one goes to Village Home, students are trusted to choose classes based on their interests.

You want to be a Chemist? We have a chemistry class.

You want to be an author? We have literature classes.

Politician? Done deal.

Historian? No problem.

At Village Home, we do not have knowledge blasting at us like a fire hose. We, the learners, are the ones who light a spark within ourselves that ignites the fire of knowledge.

When I was in public school, I was never given a choice as to what I wanted to learn. They would always teach you everything, no matter how menial or useless it seemed. Take math as an example. In public school, they would teach long math processes instead of focusing on the concept and teaching you many ways to approach solving the problem, including awesome shortcuts to make math easier. An interesting side note, shortcuts in the public school I went to had the loving pet name of "cheating!"

Another thing I remember vividly from my public school days was the endless stream of tests. At the end of the school year especially, the tests seemed like they would never end. The language arts class was the toughest for me. Between the pop quizzes and the tests in that subject alone, I had over 122 pages of tests, quizzes, pop quizzes, evaluations, essays, and reading proficiency reports. This folder that I am holding contains all of the tests that I have taken at Village Home. (At this point, he picked up his prop and opened it toward the audience, pausing for effect.) No tests. Absolutely none! Now some critics might say, "Why would you have no tests?! How can the children learn without the evaluations? And, without grades, what incentives would they have to learn?"

Firstly, do you call fear of failure incentive? In my opinion, and in the opinion of anyone you ask, fear is a terrible way of maintaining control, used by the worst tyrants in history. In public school, I was shamed into obedience and told that if my test scores were low, I would never amount to anything. At Village Home, we never have to worry about that. At Village Home, I am learning a lot, but the most important thing I am learning is that I am more than a number. I am supported and accepted. I want to work hard and learn, and I am taking responsibility for my own education and my own future. When I finish at Village, I plan to go to college to study the space frontier. I feel lucky to be studying now in an education frontier. I know that my dreams and aspirations will always be valued.

A year or so ago, I worked with one of the learners from Village on a video I needed to create. Although only sixteen years of age, this young man was very confident and skilled in the art of film production. Recently, I hired another learner to assist me with the design of promotional materials for workshops, and this book cover was designed by a fourteen-year-old young man who attends Village Home as well. It feels great to experience this reverse-mentoring, for whether we accept it or not, wisdom knows no age.

Observing how these passionate learners take charge of their lives is *really* impressive. It seems to me that their love for learning, along with their freedom to choose what they want to pursue, has given them a real growth edge for a fulfilling life. There are over twenty-nine colleges and universities, many of them Ivy League, in which the Village Home learners have matriculated. Several have leveraged their time by entering a community college at age sixteen, accomplishing their high school credential along with their associate degree. All this, along with the portfolio each has developed from an early age to highlight their accomplishments, gives them a head start with even more credit hours once they enter the baccalaureate college of their choosing, some even with a full scholarship ride. Because these learners have taken ownership of their education, many of them are able to pursue college-level courses before they are eighteen. More youth could take this path if they were given the time and space to determine who they are and what they are most curious about—and then be supported with mentors who could help guide their learning journeys. They could take a year between high school and college to learn, or be one of the many who have found a way to earn and learn simultaneously by joining a business where they can finetune a career path.

I see huge growth for Village Home as more and more parents find a way to include their role in the education of their children and become more curious about how to engage with others who share their same core values in the design of a learning community.

As the documentary *Class Dismissed* was being filmed, the producer, Jeremy Stuart, discovered Village Home and decided to make it a big part of his film. It is definitely worth seeing and perhaps sharing it and discussing it with others. There are many possibilities for how to design learning communities; and, what is needed most is for the stakeholders who have a vested interest to open up the discussion to include all the voices, especially the youth, in determining the new models. Village Home has discovered some answers that many are asking, and there may be more fertile grounds for new seeds to grow.

There are many resources coming together to help education evolve into the twenty-first century. I see it as a collaborative effort where learners of all ages stop thinking that education as a domain can reform itself and to shift the current paradigm together. There must be a way to duplicate this model in other communities, following the dynamics of systems theory. After all, it did start with one family, and now it has grown to three campuses. I believe there are conscious businesses that would say, "Please send me some of these learners to intern and learn our business." I can even hear them whispering, "For the right fit, we will help fund scholarships for the degree needed to fully maximize this career path with our organization." Who would be interested in co-creating and helping sustain this model? Might it even be a business that would venture into having a campus like this on site, which could be an employee benefit? I bet there are forward-thinking companies who just might see this as part of their sustainability strategy. The future lies in the choices we make today. Who is ready to truly start trusting the positive seeds of change?

Cultivating Fertile Learning Environments
The Pavilion: A 21ˢᵗ Century Hub for Healthy, Conscious Living

IMAGINE A 75,000-SQUARE-FOOT World's Fair-like attraction—a kind of Disneyland of healthy, conscious living—that can begin to support our communities with the latest tools, technology, and information that people need to live healthier, happier, more meaningful lives. Where people can come together to expand their minds, rejuvenate their bodies, and nourish their souls. That's *The Pavilion.*

Here, those seeking answers beyond mainstream solutions will find substance to support their "early adopter" quests. *The Pavilion's* mission is focused on serving and supporting the 70% of people over age forty-five who are suffering with chronic illness; the 38% of the population using complementary or alternative medicine; the 17% of the population interested in LOHAS (Lifestyles of Health and Sustainability); and the 33% of the population—mostly millennials—who consider themselves spiritual, but not religious, and are looking for deeper connections and meaning in their lives. Though many of these people don't crowd the health clubs, they absolutely choose to slow down the aging process with their health-driven mindset, and often steer clear of the pharmaceutical, symptom-stomping model of *sickness care,* preferring more natural approaches instead.

Other emerging trends that will be integrated into *The Pavilion's* programming include serving up "food as medicine," mindfulness practices, and the move to an updated, quantum physics model of reality—our Operating System, if you will—that is far more capable than the conventional, twenty-first-century-based science still being taught. Add to that fitness classes, a full, integrative medical and dental facility that works closely with the spa's energy medicine and anti-aging therapies, a Learning & Arts Center, a *Life Sciences "Innovation" Center*, plus weekly TED™-like talks—and you get the big, World's Fair picture of what "well-being" can look like.

The Pavilion helps people to go beyond the mundane—to *reimagine* themselves so they can live the best lives possible. According to founder, Jim Grapek, two major problems ultimately led him to develop *The Pavilion* solution. One was that humanity's emotional progress—our "emotional intelligence"—was lagging too far behind our technological progress. The other was that breathtaking advances in science were not making it out to the public—advances which would not only enable us to solve our most pressing challenges and create a more desirable future, but could help boost our emotional intelligence, as well, by bridging science and spirituality.

"These are *Copernican*-size discoveries," says Grapek, "and they give us a whole new set of possibilities. Most importantly, they greatly expand our understanding of *what's possible,* given the confirmed fact that we are both *matter* and *energy* at the same time. For example, whenever you focus your *attention* on something—by that, I mean the energy of your thoughts and conscious mind—you quite literally affect it. And the more time you spend training your 'inner self-management' skills, as physicist and Stanford Professor Emeritus William A. Tiller calls them, the more *robustly* you can affect the physical world, and you don't even have to lift a finger. Whether you're looking for a job, or better grades, or to heal from disease, honing your natural energetic abilities will greatly improve your chances for success. Up until now, Western society has mainly focused on the physical, material world. Yet, from the discovery of quantum mechanics in the 1900's right up to today, scientific understandings have dramatically changed, as one would expect. While conventional Newtonian physics still works well for things like engineering, it's been largely replaced in the scientific community by *quantum mechanics* and newer physics, because these more accurately represent how our world—and you and I—actually functions. This is a big deal, because these paradigm shifting discoveries—which also happen to be responsible for our digital revolution—show we're each capable of an extraordinary new set of abilities if we can just slow down for a few minutes to mindfully learn them. Given how the world seems to be falling apart all around us, thousands of people envisioning and co-creating a healthier future may be just the solution we're looking for."

If all goes well, *The Pavilion,* bridging many domains, will catapult people into a new mindscape and a higher level of well-being—cultivating the integration of learning and inspiration with optimal health and natural healing in an environment that is grounded in the guiding principles of this expanded, *natural* science. (I'm using the word 'natural' here because this quantum-based science is much more aligned with how Nature works than conventional science.)

The core team that's brought their own 'zones of genius' to the concept has expertise in science, BioGeometry™, architecture, media, technology, law, science, business, health, medicine, holistic education, and sustainable, balanced living. Forward-thinking, independent partners will provide services in some of these arenas and will team with management to create synergistic, community-oriented programming.

Personally, I love how this project bridges many domains with the intention of working together in a spirit of cooperation rather than competition. There's also an energy of deepening relationships, between people and the world at large—based around principles of creating abundance for all and the teachings of Rudolph Steiner, Viktor Frankl, and other such luminaries.

This vision is attracting integral thought leaders who choose to collaborate in designing a relational pathway for upgrading our learning, healing, and living systems. As these innovators begin to design open systems for educating and empowering people, they will become more resourceful in forwarding a higher quality of life. Technology plays an important role, too, as you can see with *WEB MD* and the *Health and Healing Network*. Yet, it's really about empowering people, enabling them to connect and share, and to take more active roles in shaping their lives and their successes.

By integrating internships and apprenticeships, *The Pavilion* hopes to bring forward the "seeds of change" for healthier, more conscious lifestyles, by engaging everyone—especially our youth—to become part of the process. Similarly, in the *Life Sciences Center*, mentoring programs will help provide a natural way to learn... to be inspired... and to deepen the cross-pollination between the domains, which is the hallmark of our unified (as in *holistic*), interconnected universe.

As Dennis Merritt Jones writes in his book *The Art of Abundance*, "There is no more exquisite example of the law of expansion in action and how it works than in Mother Nature herself." He gives the example of a large ear of corn that has about 800 kernels on each cornstalk which has two ears. If we assume every kernel, or seed, grows into an ear of corn – then the third generation will produce 2,560,000 cornstalks (or 4,096,000,000 kernels).

If this intelligence lives in a seed of corn, doesn't it make sense that that it exists within every living thing? As *The Pavilion* team focuses on tapping into this natural wisdom and engages our youth, as well, I predict that its future—and our future—will be healthier, happier, and brighter for everyone.

Cross-pollinating Domains
It's All About Listening

JEFF GOEBEL, THE founder of AboutListening.com, has followed his calling, and it wasn't exactly a straight and narrow path. After initially earning his bachelor's degree in Natural Resource Management at Washington State University (where he also got his master's degree in Regional Planning), he started his doctoral studies at Portland State University, pursuing Public Administration and Policy. It was at this point that he learned he had a reading disability. To hear him tell this story, I felt his frustration with the system that even though he met the American Disability Act definition of a reading disability, the system was not willing to be adaptive, and it forced him to find another way. Since then, he has pursued his passion to find solutions to problems that the so-called experts could not see.

In Jeff's own words: "It was in 1985. I remember like it was yesterday. I was standing by the Palouse Falls in SE Washington State. At that time, I worked with the USDA Soil Conservation Service, now called the Natural Resource Conservation Service (NRCS), that was celebrating over fifty years of service. As I was looking at the falls, I saw the sediment gushing over the falls so much that it was alarming to see that this overflow was losing up to two bushels of soil for every bushel of wheat production! And, to my amazement, here they were celebrating their five decades of accomplishments. I said to myself, 'There has got to be a better way!'"

So, Jeff has spent the past three decades in search of answers to extremely complex challenges revolving around this question: "How can we create and implement more regenerative, holistic solutions with our human presence on Earth?" It was this inquiry that mobilized his research concerning innovative problem solving and creating consensus. He became very adept at observing and listening, asking the best right questions, and then noticing the diversity of answers and hearing the differences. It became very apparent what was missing: a way to generate consensus through active and full participation.

In his words, "When approaching solutions to big problems, it is imperative to develop a solution in which *no one* disagrees with the decision. The deep understanding comes from the willingness to hear all of the voices, not just those who are 'for' and those who are 'against.' In this way, the marginalized perspectives are no longer marginalized." His expertise has been pursued globally through his work with the U.S. Agency for International Development (USAID), and the United Nations Food and Agriculture Organization (FAO). He has also served on a panel in the People's Climate Summit at the Paris Accord with the group Regenerative International.

Combining his research, the mentoring he has received from some of the best holistic thinkers and his thoughtful application through his own practice, he has designed a program called the Community Consensus Institute. The process works in many domains, and he has opened up new possibilities for people to move beyond conflict with a consensus approach that deepens trusting relationships that become self-renewing.

The Community Consensus Institute opens people up through deep listening and generating pathways to rebuild communities. Through this work, he has been very effective in facilitating solutions within conservation districts, corporate settings, universities, ranching and holistic land management, and with indigenous nations. He has investigated, advocated, and helped to implement regenerative solutions in many areas of human activity such as transport, housing, community development, food production, water treatment, sustainable production and consumption, and education. With his eclectic perspective, honed by time spent time as an academic, grassroots activist, business consultant, educator, and facilitator for public authorities at the local, national, and international level, Jeff is uniquely able to create systemic, renewable change.

One amazing project that demonstrates what is possible by building consensus within community is the work he did with the Colville Tribe over four years in the early 1990s. Jeff was hired by the Natural Resource Department as the Integrated Resource Management Planning (IRMP) Coordinator because the timber sales weren't getting done in a timely manner due to environmental and cultural conflict, impacting the tribal government's budget. At the time, the membership was 7,000 with the tribal government overseeing 250 programs with a $55 million annual budget. The entire tribal enterprises was generating $250 million per year.

Jeff began in his first year involving elders and community in listening, holistic goal-setting, planning, decision-making, and evaluation. As a result, they were able to create a partnership with government natural resource planners. By aligning efforts, they were able to cut more trees than foresters hoped for, while constructing two-thirds less miles of costly and environmentally damaging roads. Other accomplishments included bringing the medicine plants back, changing the concept of clearcutting to incorporate the elders' values of sustainability with nature, and reducing the treatment costs. The neighboring U.S. Forest Service lands typically did this work for $125-$300 per acre. The tribe, given the elders' input, was able to budget $75 per acre and actually do the work for only $29 per acre. Because the conflicts were resolved, Jeff and his team turned to strategic planning. Bigger results followed when they were able, within a year, to double land treatment from 10,000 acres per year to 20,000 acres at a higher cultural and environment standard while dropping the annual department budget from $17 million to $16 million.

Leveraging this success, the Tribal Business Council asked Jeff if he could do similar value added work with the whole tribal government's budget using holistic financial planning. So, in 1995-1996, Jeff led a holistic financial planning course for sixty-five of the top tribal leaders. They all agreed to the following intentions up front:

- Have unanimous agreement amongst 250 government programs and the fourteen council members as to the final budget
- Get the budget done three months early
- No job loss, no cuts in salaries, no sacred programs (like children or elders) cut
- Reduce budget by $4 million (out of $55 million)

In the end, every stipulation was met, except they were able to cut $16 million out of $55 million projected expense budget!

Not bad! When Jeff moved on to a statewide project after four years with the tribe, he realized that all of the resolutions for which he asked for Council support passed unanimously! Consensus! This was very unusual at any time, let alone consistently over four years.

There is even more good news that emerged from this project. The U.S. Senate requested Jeff's assistance with drafting three federal laws that dealt with all 550 tribes and natural resources. As a result, their recommendations became United States law.

Whenever I hear people start addressing money issues with a microscopic budgeting process—without first understanding the higher possibilities that would be revealed with the art of listening to all voices up front and seeking resolutions that would generate

100% agreement—I think of this story. Imagine the ripple effect that continues over time when there is a commitment for all of the parties involved.

For example, what's happened since 1996 for this community that reached consensus? Here's a sampling of how cross-pollination of the domains has unfolded up until today:

1. All three languages are being preserved by being transferred to young people. When Jeff was there, only 114 elders could speak any of the three languages, meaning the languages were on their way to becoming extinct! Today, all three languages have active submersion programs, which have become a model for other tribes. The elders learned that Washington State restricted elders from teaching to children in the public schools without a state university-issued teaching certificate, which the elders were successful in changing to let tribal elders have the ability to teach their children without having to go through a disrespectful process of state education (which denigrates their own cultural educational awareness).

2. The tribe invested heavily in educating their young people. Twenty years later, instead a majority of tribal members only having technical school degrees, many have master's degrees and several have PhDs.

3. The tribe acquired 100,000+ acres, making their land base the size of the state of Delaware.

4. The elders wanted to make the forests "burnable" again. Jeff and his team set out to do that by design. In the summer of 2016, a catastrophic fire swept burning 250,000 acres of tribal lands as well as U.S. Forest Service lands. The Forest Service suffered 100% stand replacement fires, meaning all of the trees were burned. The tribe only had 15-20% stand replacement fires, which meant that 80-85% of the forest remained intact.

What makes Jeff's approach unique is that he designs a safe environment where people experience the ability to see actions and the changes around them from a systemic perspective, and the wisdom to evaluate any proposed solutions in the context of their effects on the health and resilience of life as a whole. Without a holistic view, even intentional attempts to create regenerative sustainability can have ill-fated results.

We are dealing with the complexity of a profound societal change and the transition towards diverse regenerative cultures as manifestations of not only a different way of being in the world, but also a different way of seeing the world. Jeff shared with me that he was influenced by the physicist Fritjof Capra, who clearly articulated something that Jeff had intuitively known and was trying to understand better—that the "ecological, environmental, social and economic crises we are facing are not separate but interconnected expressions of one single crisis: a crisis of perception."

No matter the issues, or the people involved, it's clear we are in a process—a new evolution of our humanity. We can generate new ways of being, but it will require a shift in consciousness. It will require being comfortable with not knowing and not having the answer in advance. It does require a new listening where we can listen patiently as people disclose their truth. This also includes the need to be better attuned to our inner voices. Voicing and hearing the situation from multiple perspectives generates questions for the facilitator to guide the way. Since fear and limiting beliefs are usually the biggest obstacles, Jeff provides a safe place for all sides to be heard. His process uncovers the worst possible outcomes and the best possible outcomes (in that order); and then potential solutions naturally emerge with every participant's voice being heard.

Without this process, we just might be chasing a mirage of certainty in a profoundly ambiguous and unpredictable world. I am reminded that the answers are in the room, but only if we ask the right questions. And all views are vital to a successful, consensual solution.

And at the same time, we need to double-check our assumptions. Duane Elgin, author of several books, speaker, educator, consultant, and media activist, influenced Jeff with the idea that we ought to be very careful that we know too much. He invokes us to consider how much does science really know? Duane's thirty years of research at Stanford as a physicist led him to believe that modern science only knows 4% of the universe. What if the indigenous elders know at least 51%?

Perhaps this is one of the many reasons Jeff has worked with and learned from the indigenous people for many years. They understand Earth wisdom and have from the beginning. As a matter of fact, all first nations people around the world have warned for years that we must change our ways in order to live in harmony with the Earth. There are talking circles with Native leaders voicing the prophecies of destruction unless we begin to relate harmoniously with Mother Earth. (I co-produced a video of these talking circles, and it is alive and well as a teaching tool at PullTogetherNow. com) Some non-natives are listening, but certainly not enough.

In a recent conversation with Jeff, he shared that back in 2011, he felt he was on the final stretch of his life and he wondered to himself, "What is the biggest global problem that needs solving to help my grandchildren's future?" Being quiet and listening to his inner voice, Jeff heard the answer: climate change. So, for the past eight years, he has been working to model, teach, and duplicate consensus building with the purpose of getting people to listen in order to cross-pollinate the domains and foster regenerative solutions. According to Jeff: "We need to listen to the land, as it will teach us more than people; and we will become more curious about our world. As citizens of planet Earth, we all are participants and our future depends on a holistic perspective."

And Jeff knows that the kids are some of the most important parties. Recently, he and his daughter-in-law, Theresa Goebel, wrote and published a book titled *The One Thing You Can Do to Save the Earth*. It is a children's book, written for adults—parents and grandparents—to read to their children. Concerned about the quality of life that their own children and grandchildren will be inheriting due to a lack of holistic understanding, Jeff and Theresa bring to life how Mother Earth, as a living organism, is hurting. In the story, the children experience this wakeup call, coming from Mother Earth to all of us living during these times; and they are not shy about asking questions as they search for ways to stop the pain and suffering for all of Earth's creatures. They go on an adventure and explore what it is to become one with the "soil," and they experience the regenerative living nature of the Earth. They relate to the earthworms, to the germination of seeds, to what happens when pesticides impact the food we eat. They explore the sun and the solar cycle of photosynthesis and what happens when that is interrupted. They clearly get that the Earth will continue, but will humans survive? As a result, they make a list of ways we can all begin now to be part of the solution. They see themselves as Earth Ambassadors on a mission, and so again... "out of the mouths of babes," we discover solutions to serious challenges.

Jeff has the expertise and capacity to bring about powerful changes; and yet he is *one* person with a big dream to bridge cultural divides in order to address our common human environmental predicament. Jeff's Community Consensus Institute is designed to share his experiences and build capacity so others may help many others to solve complex issues through consensus building.

A perfect scenario would be to collaborate with a community of leaders who could design and implement a holistic model, where the different generations—including the youth—could come together to support the new sciences and willingly integrate with a regenerative approach to growing food in ways that respect the Earth's ability to continually renew herself. Conscious businesses, focusing on the quadruple bottom line of *purpose, people, profit,* and *planet,* would serve the people as they co-create regenerative lifestyles. The schools could be the meeting place for it all to begin.

Imagine every school with a garden where students grow their own healthy, nutrient-dense vegetables, pesticide-free. Designing learning around real life includes knowing where your food comes from, along with understanding how to nourish the body and how to get along with others. Building a living holistic system would include an understanding of money and how to manage resources; and it would be centered on relationships rather than transactions. You can see already that this is not based on separating the domains of knowledge. Instead, the living system model would be the guiding praxis. Integrating open-source technology would facilitate the sharing of knowledge and how to apply the learning for critical thinking, change management, innovating new programs and products for serving the new economy that will naturally emerge. With the soul of technology, there is no longer any need to compartmentalize our humanness. We can adopt a perspective of global ecology through stories, and it ultimately becomes a shared concept. This understanding reinforces inclusion, support, and the expression of gratitude for our one big planetary family.

Schools can become organic learning communities. We can connect the work to make it happen. If we don't act now to bring about the positive changes, the youth will ask us why we didn't. It only requires a small group of people to decide, and Jeff could use your help. Repair, rebuild, regenerate—working to build a relationship with nature is a good first step. Cross-pollination is a natural process if we only choose to upgrade our thinking to listen and work together for the positive changes. We either embrace change, or we will become extinct.

Sustaining with Regenerative Resources and Systems
Creating the Future

CREATING THE FUTURE IS a not-for-profit organization out of Tucson, AZ, founded in 2011 by Hildy Gottlieb and Dimitri Petropolis. The grounding for this vision came through decades of Hildy's research, idea development, and experimentation. After watching her Tedx Talk "How to Create the Future," I joined a beta program called Catalytic Thinking, which has now become a course that is a key part of their education offering.

I appreciated the stories Hildy and her Creating the Future team shared about the transformative projects they help facilitate with possibility-thinking. One of their core tenets is that "together we have everything we need—it is only on our own that we experience scarcity." Moving people away from "What's wrong?" to "What's right?" helps bring out the best in people.

Their second tenet is "the most favorable conditions begin and end with bringing out the best in people versus focusing on stuff (money, food, education, etc.)."

By following the Catalytic Thinking principles, we are empowered to lead from the middle. We don't need positional authority. The secret is asking a different question, and then observing what opens up as a result. Creating the Future's team encourages us to rethink the assumptions that are driving our current actions.

I noticed that people who practiced the principles became more courageous in their conversations.

For Hildy, the goal of her work is "to determine how much more humane the world could be if the questions embedded in all of the systems everywhere, were bringing out the best in each other."

The bottom line: Change the Questions, Change the World!

The scientific research she and her team share concerning the brain and how language impacts reactionary or creative responses helps people become more conscious of their choices. This platform offers people a meeting place for real change to happen in families, schools, businesses, non-profit organizations, social services, and even countries.

Creating the Future is now a collection of people around the world, putting that catalytic thinking into action, in a ten-year experiment in systems change and bringing out the best in everyone around them.

The focus is on creating systems that encourage creativity and compassion through embodying the awareness of "collective enoughness." Believe me, this is *not* strategic planning, which is normally short-term. This is about understanding change—how it happens and how it matters for the long-term. Instead of talking about what we don't want in our world (poverty, guns, terrorism, etc.), what kind of world do we really want? What path will lead us there? Who else cares about this?

Courageous and confident, Creating the Future's team began this experiment in 2016. By 2026, they envision a positive shift. Modeling the systems thinking on a huge scale, they have organized resources and opened sharing to have experimenters demonstrate and share stories so people can see what is working and perhaps apply what they learn to their own situations. I love that they have "Convening and Building Community" as one of their core intentions for this ten-year journey. What better way could there be for people to learn, grow, and support each other, and at the same time have a safe place to practice a more integral way of being?

When I get curious about what might be missing for this grand vision to become the paradigm shift it's called to bring forth, my answer is, "Find a way to include the youth." What if we design an internship model and then replicate that in a way that will engage the youth to become an essential part of the unfoldment? They are the leaders of our future, so I imagine core intergenerational teams that connect in different cities and with smart technology and video production, including documentaries. Another key question I would ask is: How might internships become apprenticeships for presenting conscious leadership for the twenty-first century, and how might we leverage the soul of technology along the way?

Reaching Upward and Beyond with Technology
Innovators

A COMPANY THAT impresses me about their focus on youth and learning with technology is Elemental Path, co-founded by CEO Donald Coolidge. Their mission is to improve the way kids learn by improving the way they play. He and his team have created the first kid-oriented artificial intelligence smart toy that is really more of a companion than a toy. Branded as CogniToys, they are powered by their cloud-based personality engine that enables "easy creation of custom speech-based personalities." What makes this line totally unique is that where other smart toys rely on pre-programmed responses, their "Friendgine-powered dinosaurs listen to kids' questions and adapt to their age, allowing them to grow over time — just like kids do." The CogniToys can answer each child's questions, tell bedtime stories, and can even tell jokes. Their latest called STEMosaur comes as a kit that includes the parts including a kid friendly code panel that can be personalized.

The kids get to learn the engineering and the coding that makes it work. And when they are finished, they have a creation that they designed that can carry on a normal conversation. In their words: "We are enabling (kids) to have more interactive and engaging play experiences that are rooted in educational content."

This, of course, will likely affect their participation in the new economy of Makers.

The Maker's Movement is coming on strong as millions of people are inventing their creative designs, turning them into self-made products, and starting businesses in which to sell them on line. Take Etsy, for example. In his Huffington Post article, "What is the Maker Movement and Why Should You Care?", Brit Morin says, "In a world of modern technology, it has made it easier than ever for single individuals to create and distribute items that are customizable and unique without having middlemen like manufacturers. This growing shift will continue to affect the economy and will likely have big implications on large retailers. It is a special time in history that will have a transformative impact on our future." And T.J. McCue, contributor to *Forbes* agrees, "Makers—people who create, build, design, tinker, modify, hack, invent, or simply make something—are on the rise and are moving the economy."

In both Elemental Path and the Maker's Movement, I can see how trusting the seeds of change with their innovative approach and engaging the wisdom of the youth as co-designers is at the core; and I wonder how they will cross-pollinate the domains of knowledge as they grow their interactive content and find new ways of connecting with consumers.

To bring forward the idea of learning as a creative act, it would be a path for youth to have a crack at product-oriented learning. Of course, one way to do that would be to bring the Maker Movement into schools. Youth seem to light up when they are able to develop skills that have a real world connection, and especially when they are more in control of what they are learning in terms of a project rather than working on projects that their teacher designed.

In an entrepreneurial model, the learner would need to convince the teacher of the idea, and perhaps convince a team of peers to be partners. In this scenario, the teacher would assume the role of a venture capitalist and decide if the project is needed and feasible. This would be truly flipping the classroom, and with the use of technology—where the universe can be found on Google—a whole new way of learning can take hold.

Integrating technology in ways that build these skills through collaboration will definitely require new ways of relating with teachers. Wouldn't this be soulful work?

A Special Invitation
Live The Potential with Us!

THERE HAS NEVER been a more important time for us to come together for our children and our world, and we are better together. As a parent, a teacher, a business executive or entrepreneur, a technology expert, or a leader in your community, you are probably asking, "What's next? Where can I plant and cultivate my own seeds of genius on behalf of the children and the planet? How can I be part of this change that is so needed?"

I have been asked this question so many times that I have developed a quick and easy tool to help us help *you* find your place in this movement and network you with the right people and organizations.

Once you answer the survey questions, my team will reach out to you to set up a time to locate your perfect place in this network, or possibly even one of the amazing programs we have created to train facilitators to bring this new approach into their communities.

Please bring your seeds of genius over to Living The Potential Network! Become part of a growing community that is committed to cultivating fertile learning environments, cross-pollinating the domains of education and business, creating sustainability, and reaching upward and beyond with the soul of technology.

Together, we can engage the wisdom of our youth and save the world!

Take the Assessment to Get Started!
www.LivingThePotentialNetwork.com

About Renee Beth

RENEE BETH POINDEXTER is the founder of Living The Potential Network, a growing collaborative of social entrepreneurs interested in designing authentic learning environments. Her breakthrough mentorship program helps self-starting, entrepreneurial parents and growth-minded teachers engage the wisdom of the youth to save the world alongside forward-thinking businesses.

Accomplished trainer, facilitator, success coach, and organizational consultant, Renee Beth discovered the significance of learning in the world of business over twenty-five years—across many sectors, including technology, healthcare, financial services, construction, advertising and public relations, executive search, coaching, and consulting. A former high school English teacher, Renee Beth has worked with non-profit organizations, schools, and businesses to facilitate the positive changes needed to fulfill their organizational vision. Her background in continuous improvement has assisted her in designing programs that inspire people to lead with their heads and hearts connected and create better results.

Renee Beth's current work through Living The Potential Network includes coaching, consulting, and mentoring social entrepreneurs who are courageously choosing to own their purpose and design their legacy with one common goal: Leave the world better than we found it.

Her book, *Living The Potential: Engaging the Wisdom of Our Youth to Save the World*, invites people who are vested in a positive future to open new pathways for collaboration—where everyone can bring more of who we are to what we do and how we do it, and engage the wisdom of our youth as active participants in co-creating a happier, healthier future for all.

Renee Beth is a frequent guest host for Pathways, a radio show for personal and cultural transformation streamed globally on KBOO-FM. She is Chair of the SelfDesign Foundation in the United States, and has served as an Advisory Board member with Univera, Inc. and currently with Village Home Education Resource Center.

A global traveler, Renee Beth makes her home in Portland, Oregon, with her husband, Mark Roth. She loves people, nature, and adventure and is a master networker.

Resources

Chapter One

"Addiction by the Numbers." Center on Addiction. https://www.centeronaddiction.org

Atkins, Alexander. "How Many College Grads Have Jobs Related to Their Major?" *Abookshelfz*. https://atkinsbookshelf.wordpress.com/2016/03/03/how-many-college-grads-have-jobs-related-to-their-major/ Accessed February 6, 2019.

Bares, Ann. "Compensation Force: Practical News, information, tips about employee performance and compensation" February 5, 2014.

http://www.compensationforce.com/2014/02/2013-turnover-rates-by-industry.html
Accessed December 26, 2018.

Eberly, Janice C. and James H. Stock. *Brookings Papers on Economic Activity Spring 2016.* The Brookings Press, 2016.

Ibid. Brookings Papers on Economic Activity Fall 2016. The Brookings Press, 2016.

Graham, Carol. *Happiness for All? Unequal Lives and Hopes in the Land of the Dream.* Princeton University Press, 2017.

Kamenetz, Anya. "The Truth About America's Graduation Rate: From 'Dropout Crisis' to Record High, Dissecting the Graduation Rate." June 12, 2015. www.wbgo.org/people/anya-kamenetz. Accessed February 6, 2019.

Kenny, Charles. Results Not Receipts: Counting the Right Things in Aid and Corruption. Center for Global Development. CBD Brief 2017. https://www.cgdev.org/sites/default/files/Results-Not-Receipts-Brief.pdf Accessed February 6, 2019.

Pacer Center: Champions for Children with Disabilities. Bullying Prevention. https://www.pacer.org/publications/bullying.aspPacer.org Accessed February 6, 2019.

Partnership for Drug-Free Kids. Teen Substance Abuse. https://drugfree.org/search_gcse/?ss360Query=Teen%20Substance%20Abuse

Taylor Protocols' Core Value Index. The Core Values Index is the only assessment to showcase the core motivational drivers that dictate performance. These drivers dictate the behaviors and desired work that develop self-esteem, causing people to subconsciously seek work where they can make their highest contribution. https://www.taylorprotocolsinc.com/how-the-cvi-works

The Parent Resource Program: The Jason Foundation. "Youth Suicide Statistics." http://jasonfoundation. com/get-involved/parent/parent-resource-program/

Chapter Two

Declaration of Learners Rights and Responsiblities. Cameron, Brent and River Meyer Unfolding Our Infinite Wisdom Within. SelfDesign Learning Systems Inc, 2012.

(Has also been published by UNESCO and has been distributed in newsletters and magazines in at least 10 countries around the world)

Dweck, Carol, PhD. *Mindset: The New Psychology of Success.* Ballantine Books, 2007.

Gupta, James. "10 Surprising Facts About Your Memory." Medium. October 30, 2017. https://medium. com/@gupta_james/10-surprising-facts-about-your-memory-7666d61600b9

Gupta, James. blog.synap.ac/author/james-gupta

Sousa, David. *How the Brain Learns.* Corwin; Fifth edition, 2016.

Chapter Three

"The Future of Jobs." *World Economic Forum.* http:// reports.weforum.org/future-of-jobs-2016/. Accessed December 27, 2018.

Chapter Four

Econet. Econetholdings.com

Chapter Five

Friedman, Thomas. *Thank You for Being Late: An Optimist's Guide to Thriving in the Age of Accelerations.* Picadour, 2017.

Goleman, Daniel. Emotional Intelligence: A Practical Guide to Making Friends with Your Emotions and Raising Your EQ (Positive Psychology Coaching Series Book 8) CreateSpace Independent Publishing Platform, 2015.

Mitra, Sugitra. "We Need Schools...Not Factories." *Huffington Post.* April 29, 2018. https://www.huffingtonpost.com/sugata-mitra/2013-ted-prize_b_2767598.html. Accessed December 22, 2018.

Pink, Daniel. *A Whole New Mind: Moving from the Information Age to the Conceptual Age.* Riverhead Books, 2006.

The SelfDesign Mandala. Cameron, Brent and River Meyer. *SelfDesign: Unfolding Our Infinite Wisdom Within.* SelfDesign Learning Systems Inc. color edition, 2012.

The Movement Has Begun

Goebel, Jeff and Theresa Goebel. *The One Thing You Can Do to Save the Earth*. Blurb, 2017.

Jones, Dennis Merritt. *The Art of Abundance: Ten Rules for a Prosperous Life.* Tarcher Perigee, 2018.

Morin, Brit. "What is the Maker Movement and Why Should You Care?" Huffington Post. 05/02/2013 https://www.huffingtonpost.com/brit-morin/what-is-the-maker-movemen_b_3201977.html. Accessed December 27, 2018.

Made in the USA
San Bernardino, CA
29 March 2019